THE WALLACE CON[

The Story of the Restoration of Orford Church

The union of two Orford clerical families, the Scotts and the Maynards:
the wedding of Malcolm Scott and Bessie Maynard, 1898
Back row from left Miss Mary Scott, John Murray Scott, Mrs Mary Scott (wife of Douglas),
three bridesmaids (the third is Miss Mary Maynard), General Douglas Scott,
unidentified bridesmaid, Mrs Ida Scott (wife of Edward), Revd Edward Scott,
Miss Alicia Scott, Dr John Maynard, Revd Charles Raymond
Middle row from left Kathleen Scott, Mrs Louisa Maynard (the bride's mother),
Malcolm Scott, Bessie Scott, Mrs Alicia Scott (the groom's mother), Walter Scott
At front Ruth Scott, Brida Scott

The Wallace Connection

The Story of the Restoration of Orford Church

Jane Allen

ORFORD MUSEUM
2008

Published by Orford Museum
(Reg. Charity No. 1052307)
Bell House Quay Street Orford
Woodbridge Suffolk IP12 2NU

ISBN 978-0-9554738-0-7

Prepared for publication by Agnesi Text, Hadleigh
Printed in England by EAM Printers, Ipswich

Also published by Orford Museum

*The Building of Orford Castle:
A Translation from the Pipe Rolls 1163–78*
by Valerie Potter, Margaret Poulter and Jane Allen (2002)

Thanks to generous support from the Scarfe Charitable Trust
and other donors, all the proceeds of the sale of this book
will be divided between
the St Bartholomew's Church Restoration Appeal Fund
and the funds of Orford Museum.

Contents

List of Illustrations

FRONT COVER

Orford church from the south (detail)

(Photo by Alan Blair)

Images of Sir Richard and Lady Wallace, John Murray Scott and Edward Scott:
detail of photograph on p. 47

(New Orford Town Trust/Orford Museum)

BACK COVER

East end of Orford church seen through the 'Scott' memorial screen

(Photo by Jane Lennox)

Acknowledgements

I am not quite sure at what point my notes for a one-hour talk about the restoration of St Bartholomew's church in the late nineteenth century began to turn into a book. The impetus almost certainly came from the ever-growing volume of material that came my way once it became known that I was interested in the subject.

First and foremost I must thank Nigel Sheffield, a direct descendant of both of the clerical families, Maynards and Scotts, who feature in this book. He is a great nephew of the Revd Edward Scott and Sir John Murray Scott and he answered my many impertinent questions about his family's business with good humour, generosity and, partly due to his grandmother's remarkable longevity (she died in her 104th year in 1975), authority. He allowed me a free run of the album of family photographs taken in the 1920s by his mother Gillie, the daughter of Malcolm Scott and Bessie Maynard, and it is these photographs which bring the book to life. It was my friends Valerie and Julian Potter who introduced me to Nigel and who also offered me advice and encouragement when the project 'sagged' for a year or two after I had done the initial writing job. I am very grateful to them.

Another, more remote, family connection of the Scotts was the late Dr Peter Cardew whose father was Edward Scott's successor as rector of Orford. Peter produced a family tree and photographs. His nephew Martin Cardew, also very knowledgeable about the Scott family, was able to put me right on a number of points, identify almost everyone in the frontispiece photograph and provide some valuable additional information, especially about the musical talents of the family.

There is always an element of serendipity in any enterprise, and in the case of this book it was when Mrs Hazel Villier wrote out of the blue with a photograph of Birkdale, the house in Branksome to which Edward Scott and his family retired, thus shedding some welcome light on the years 'after Orford'. An enquiry sent to Orford rectory at about the same time by Mrs Jacqueline Hargest, a descendant of Edward Scott's wife, Ida, was another happy coincidence.

I was enormously helped by a number of museum and library 'professionals', not least by Margaret Poulter, honorary curator of Orford Museum. She has patiently responded to all my requests for information and her meticulous cataloguing of the museum's excellent collection of drawings and photographs made picture research for this book a pleasure.

Andrea Gilbert of the Wallace Collection Library, Nick Clarke at the Britten–Pears Library, the archivist at the Birmingham City Archives, Cicely Greenhill of the

Society for the Protection of Ancient Buildings and Clare Brown at Lambeth Palace Library, where the archive of the Incorporated Church Building Society is held, were very helpful and produced information which I could never have found for myself. One of the most satisfying outcomes of my enquiries was the visit made to Orford church by Ann Eatwell of the department of sculpture, metalwork, ceramics and glass at the Victoria and Albert Museum. I asked her to help me to identify the makers of the brass ornaments and furnishings which were bestowed on the church in quantity as part of Edward Scott's restoration. This she did, but she went away having discovered that St Bartholomew's, Orford, possessed a very fine and rare set of late eighteenth-century silver communion plate made by Matthew Boulton and John Fothergill. It is now on loan to the new Gallery of Sacred Silver and Stained Glass at the V&A.

I have been helped by many friends in Orford and elsewhere: Canon Norman Davis, Tim Fargher, Bill and Jane Lennox, Alexandra Paton, Richard Power (who drew the maps) and Geoffrey Smeed who patiently took innumerable photographs in Orford and Sudbourne churches. I have also used photos taken by Patrick Cannell and Charles Salisbury. The churchwardens and Parochial Church Councils of both Orford and Sudbourne have given permission for me to photograph and use pictures from their churches.

The New Orford Town Trust has been similarly co-operative.

The late John Anderson allowed me to use a number of items from the album of press-cuttings and photographs compiled by his grandfather, Lou Anderson, which David Andren photographed, and Spinny Bantoft lent me his bound copy of the Sudbourne and Orford parish magazines of 1888.

I must especially thank Jack Robinson who, often to very short order, scanned very many of the images used in this book.

I have sought and obtained much good advice from a number of people who have read various drafts of the book – John and Margaret Poulter, Julian Potter, Michael Flint, Roy Tricker and especially my husband Tim.

A number of copyright holders have given permission to use pictures and quotations from various published sources, some of them, generously, without charge. I would like to acknowledge the publishers of *Apollo* magazine, the National Portrait Gallery, The Wallace Collection, the RIBA Library, Lambeth Palace Library, Aldeburgh Museum, Felicity Cambridge, Adam Nicolson, Alan Blair (photographer), John Murray Publishers for quotations from *Another Part of the Wood* by Kenneth Clark, Faber and Faber and the Britten Estate for 'The other side of the Alde' from the *Tribute to Benjamin Britten on his Fiftieth Birthday*, and Orion Publishing for *Vita, The Life of Victoria Sackville West* by Victoria Glendinning and *Portrait of a Marriage* by Nigel Nicolson.

Should I have failed to secure the necessary permissions from any other copyright-holder, or indeed forgotten to acknowledge any kind of help from the very many people who have wished this book well, I can only apologize.

I must particularly thank those who have sponsored the publication of this book, thus enabling all sales proceeds to go to the St Bartholomew's, Orford, Restoration Fund and to Orford Museum:

The Scarfe Charitable Trust, Graeme and Anna Williams, Sally Walton, John and Julia Waite, Margaret Poulter, Michael and Phyllida Flint, Tim and Elizabeth Fargher, Tom Bridges, David Andren and Tim Allen.

Finally all responsibility for errors and omissions is mine.

J.A.

Foreword

THE RIGHT REVD NIGEL STOCK, BISHOP OF ST EDMUNDSBURY AND IPSWICH

Every church restoration project is a major undertaking for the parish concerned, and sometimes quite a drama. Once the work is finished, the details and the difficulties are soon forgotten, the new work is admired and eventually taken for granted.

By unearthing the Orford Church Restoration Committee Minute Book and reading the files of the Incorporated Church Building Society and other records, Jane Allen has uncovered the whole story of the large-scale restoration of St Bartholomew's, Orford from 1892 to 1900, masterminded by a determined rector, the Revd Edward Maude Scott. The element of drama came from the connection between the rector's family and the local landowner – Sir Richard Wallace. In this respect Orford's church restoration story was far from typical.

Jane Allen is to be congratulated on producing an instructive and detailed account of a Victorian church restoration, enlivened by a remarkable and at times sensational human-interest story. The latter is, mercifully, unlikely to be encountered by modern incumbents and their congregations embarking on a programme of restoration. However I was intrigued by the famous names that emerge and to discover how the actual 'Wallace Connection' came about. Like the author, I have taken great pleasure from visits to the Wallace Collection (which began from the desire as a boy to see the original of the Laughing Cavalier). I am delighted to know that there is a link to Sudbourne and Orford.

When I was a Residentiary Canon at one of the great cathedrals of this country, I was often struck by how often records were lost as to why certain things had happened to the fabric. If this was true of such a well-documented building as a cathedral, it is even more true of the parish churches. Thanks to Jane Allen's efforts we have a fine record of one stage of the story of Orford Church.

At Orford repair and maintenance work is continuing with the energy shown by so many Suffolk parishes and the proceeds of this little book will be shared between Orford Museum and the Orford Church Restoration Fund.

✠ NIGEL ST EDMUNDSBURY & IPSWICH

Preface

The Millennium saw an exciting project at St Bartholomew's church in Orford.

It was decided to round off the work that had been done in the 1970s, when the rebuilding of the tower was completed, by restoring a full ring of bells and moving the choir vestry to the ground floor of the tower. The north-east chapel, which had been used as the priest's vestry, could be cleared, with a view to restoring it as a chapel for private prayer and weekday services.

In the course of the work, the time came to empty various cupboards in the church and that was when some interesting items came to light – the Church Restoration Committee's Minute Book from 1892 to 1915, five coloured architect's plans and drawings and all the nineteenth-century church terriers – from which a great deal of the information in this book is derived. Most have now been deposited with other parish records in the Suffolk Record Office at Ipswich.

The Millennium was rung in by Orford's new band of ringers amidst great celebrations. The following year, however, the heating boiler gave up the ghost, and the architect's quinquennial inspection in 2002 revealed serious defects in the church fabric. A Church Restoration Appeal was launched in May 2003.

For a fund-raising event held by the Friends of Orford Museum I prepared a talk about how things were done at the last major restoration campaign 110 years ago. My researches, which started with the modest aim of compiling an account of the works undertaken and church furnishings acquired at that time, soon led me to the energetic and much commemorated rector who master-minded the work, the Revd Edward Scott. I knew that through his brother, John Murray Scott, there was a connection with one of my favourite museums, the Wallace Collection.

I did not know that I would uncover quite such an interesting and at times sensational story. A contented and respectable family was thrown into some turmoil by an enormous inheritance which attracted the attention of a member of one of the oldest aristocratic families in the land and ended up in the law courts and the national press.

The mixture of local history, ecclesiology and scandal has made it great fun to write this book and I hope that it will also be fun to read.

JANE ALLEN
Bell House, Orford, July 2008

[xvii]

Introduction

St Bartholomew's church Orford, like so many others, owes much of its present appearance to the efforts of those who instituted a programme of restoration in the nineteenth century – what is usually described as the Victorian restoration. In Orford's case, the restoration process extended well beyond the Victorian period. The main structural work to the roofs and walls was begun in 1895 and completed in the remaining six years of the Queen's reign, but other work went on into the 1920s; the rood screen, choir stalls and east window were dedicated on All Saints' Day 1921 and the restored west window and new west door on 4 November 1928.

No one who visits the church today can fail to notice the numerous inscriptions which tell us that much of the work that was done was the responsibility of the Revd Edward Scott[1] and members of his family.

The windows of the south porch have the letter S incorporated into the glazing pattern and around the roof are the words, 'In the year 1900 this porch being ruinous & falling was repaired in memory of John Scott and Alicia Lucy his wife by their son rector of this parish. Thanks be to God.' The interior of the church is dominated by the large and intricately carved rood screen given, as an incised and gilded inscription tells us, 'To the glory of God and in loving memory of Edward Maude Scott born 6 September 1850 died 6 June 1917. Rector of Sudbourn and Orford 1877–1901. Erected by his wife Ida Marion Scott.' In the St Nicholas chapel the painting of the Holy Family by Rafaelino dal Colle in its Florentine-style frame above the altar is also given 'In loving memory of Edward Maude Scott priest, born September 6 1850, died June 6 1917, rector of Sudbourne cum Orford 1877–1901' and inscriptions on the brass cross ('A gift to God presented by Alicia Scott in memory of her beloved husband John Scott MD. Easter 1891'), candlesticks ('In loving memory of John Scott MD by his children. Easter 1891') and lectern ('In loving memory of our mother this lectern is presented by Alicia, Mary and Walter Scott AD 1900') show that the embellishment of that part of the church was very much a Scott family project. The large

---

General note When today's value of sums of money are given, the tables in the Bank of England's
  Equivalent contemporary values of the pound: a historical survey 1270 to 2004 are used.

1 Although every commemorative inscription to him in Orford church refers to the rector as Edward Maude Scott, within his family he was known simply as Edward, and that is the usage followed in this book.

Window in Orford church porch showing the letter S in the glazing pattern

eagle lectern in the nave was also given 'To the glory of God and in loving memory of John Scott MD. Easter 1891'. Less conspicuous is the prayer desk in the sanctuary to the left of the altar 'In memory of Phyllis Maud Scott. Easter 1893'.

Outside the church, in the east wall, there are plaques dated 1896 under the main east window and 1899 by the south-east window. To the right of the pathway leading from the ruins of the Norman chancel north to the gate in The Old Rectory wall is a square burial plot surrounded by a low iron railing where Scott family graves are to be found.

This book sets out to explain a little about the parish of Sudbourne and Orford and the appearance of Orford church before Edward Scott got to work. The wealth of material in the church records and the files of the Incorporated Church Building Society provides a detailed description of the restoration programme from the first meeting of the Orford Church Restoration Committee in 1892 up to the dedication of the rood screen in Edward Scott's memory in 1921. Subsequent repairs and works of restoration and improvement, all contributing to the appearance of the church as it is today, are also described.

Who were the Scotts, and why were they in Orford?

The answer lies in the Wallace connection.

Sir Richard Wallace's name is synonymous with the world-famous collection of magnificent paintings, furniture, porcelain and other items that is displayed in Hertford House in Manchester Square in London. The collection should really be known as the Hertford/Wallace Collection because (although he did augment it) Sir Richard Wallace inherited the collection from his natural father, the 4th Marquis of Hertford – and here lies the connection with the parish of Sudbourne and Orford.

The Marquises of Hertford had been the owners of the Sudbourne estate since 1754. Sir Richard Wallace owned it from 1872 to 1884. He employed as his secretary John Murray Scott, the older brother of the Revd Edward Scott, who, as the inscriptions tell us, became rector in 1877. Amongst many improvements in all the villages of the estate, Sir Richard Wallace paid for the virtual rebuilding of Sudbourne church in 1878–79. In 1881 he commissioned plans for the restoration of Orford church from one of the foremost architects of the day – G. E. Street (although Street's scheme was not carried out).

The Wallace connection outlived Sir Richard Wallace, who died in 1890. In fact it grew stronger, because John Murray Scott continued to work for the widowed Lady Wallace until her death in 1897. A close friendship had developed between Lady Wallace and members of the Scott family, particularly John Murray Scott's mother and sisters.

In June 1898 Edward Scott wrote to the Incorporated Church Building Society to thank them for a grant of £70 towards the second phase of the Orford church restoration project, saying 'It is very difficult to gather money nowadays.' In fact his brother, John Murray Scott, had 'gathered' a huge amount of money in the previous year as effectively the sole beneficiary of the will of Lady Wallace. Although that part of the Hertford/Wallace collection which was on the ground and first floors of Hertford House in London was left to the nation and became the Wallace Collection, the remainder of the collection, most of which was in Paris, plus property in Paris and

The Scott family graves in Orford churchyard

[3]

Lisburn in Ireland, an enormous sum of money and even the lease on Hertford House, were inherited by the rector's brother.

After John Murray Scott's death in 1913 the Scott family hit the newspaper headlines when they brought a High Court action to contest their brother's will. The events that precipitated their sudden appearance under the spotlight of the national press and which brought them within an inch of that vast fortune, but which left them with only a small fortune, are also recounted in this book.

The Scotts, and particularly another brother, Malcolm, continued to contribute generously to the repair and embellishment of Orford church for the first half of the twentieth century. Malcolm Scott's wife Bessie was the granddaughter of Revd John Maynard, Edward Scott's predecessor as rector, who had come to Orford in 1842. In fact the Maynard family's contribution to this story is almost as significant as that of the Scotts, and was of longer duration. Their gifts are not inscribed as prominently as those of the Scotts and unfortunately the lettering on their gravestones in the Norman chancel ruins has not stood the test of time and is now illegible.

In 1950 the large painting, *The Holy Family with St John and a donor* by Bernadino Luini, which hangs above the altar, was given to the church by Dr John Maynard.[2] He had received a legacy from John Murray Scott thirty-seven years earlier. The rebuilding of the tower in the 1960s was begun with a legacy from Dr Maynard's sister. It could be said that these gifts were the final strands in the Wallace connection.

2   See chapter 17, p. 127 below.

I

Sudbourne and Orford – Two Churches, One Rector

The adjoining Suffolk civil parishes of Sudbourne (sometimes spelt Sudbourn) and Orford are protected from the tidal river Ore by a river wall. On the far side of the river is the long, narrow shingle spit known as Orford Ness. Beyond Orford Ness is the North Sea.

The village of Orford is on the river. It has a quay, a market place, a church (St Bartholomew's) and a fine Norman castle, built by King Henry II between 1165 and 1173. The main part of Sudbourne village is about three miles from the river. There are a few outlying clusters of houses and the church (All Saints') stands on its own, apart from a neighbouring farm house, just over a mile south of the village.[1] Sudbourne Hall is also isolated, about equidistant from the two churches, and closer to Orford than to what is now the main part of Sudbourne village. Until the early twentieth century the Sudbourne estate encompassed Sudbourne, much of Orford, and a number of other villages, a total area of some 11,000 acres.

In the Domesday survey of 1086 the manor of Sudbourne is listed, held partly by the monastery at Ely, and partly by Robert Malet, one of William the Conqueror's barons. Malet's holding is the larger of the two. Orford is not named in Domesday Book although some of the features of Malet's holding, a mill (which in the eleventh century would have been a tide mill), a fishpond and a salt house, seem more likely to be in what is now Orford (with its quay offering facilities for a fishing fleet) than in the inland settlement of Sudbourne.

Domesday Book was compiled almost a hundred years before the royal castle and the church were built at Orford. Parish boundaries, which had for the most part become settled long before the Normans came in 1066, were not easily upset, so the new church at Orford was designated a chapel to the pre-existing mother church at Sudbourne, in spite of the fact that Orford had become the more important settlement. The parish, although it is now part of a group of parishes called the Wilford Team Ministry, is still designated 'Orford with Sudbourne' (it was only in the late twentieth century that Orford's name began to precede that of Sudbourne).

---

1   The main Sudbourne settlement developed only after the enclosure of Sudbourne Common in 1807 (see p. 24, below and Tom Williamson, *Sandlands: The Suffolk Coast and Heaths*, Windgather Press, 2005, p. 80, and Vic Harrup, 'Captain's Wood, Sudbourne', *Orford & District Local History Bulletin*, Issue 6, 2006, p. 1).

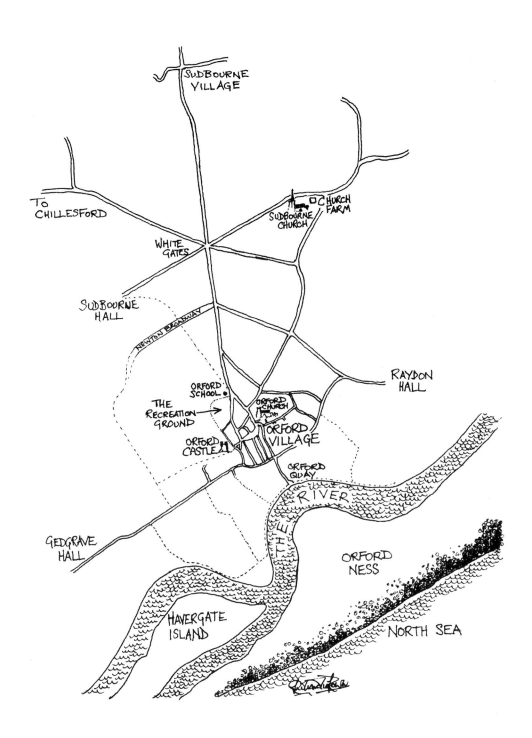

Map showing the villages of Orford and Sudbourne

It is worth noting that the 'twinning' of parish churches with a chapel is quite common on Suffolk's notoriously unstable coastline. One of the two churches in each pair is generally situated further inland than the other. They are, in addition to Sudbourne with Orford, Reydon with Southwold, Leiston with Sizewell, Aldringham with Thorpe[2] and Walberswick with Blythburgh. The 'chapels' at Orford and Southwold are much larger than their respective mother churches as the settlement right on the coast almost inevitably became the more prosperous of the two because of the commercial opportunities from fishing and shipping.[3] In Orford's case, the presence of the royal castle was undoubtedly an additional economic benefit.

At quite an early date, in just one respect Orford achieved ascendency over Sudbourne in the ecclesiastical hierarchy. The deanery of twenty-one parishes which corresponded to the civil administrative area of the Plomesgate hundred was, from the thirteenth to the twentieth century, known as the Orford deanery.[4]

The rectory for the combined parish seems to have become established in Orford, immediately to the north of the church, from an early date.[5]

The earliest maps showing Sudbourne and Orford are coastal charts, so the features marked are those which could be landmarks – trees, church towers, windmills, beacons and conspicuous buildings. A chart, thought to date from 1570–80,[6] shows a house called Chapmans at the site of Sudbourne Hall. Nearby is a building marked as the Lazar House (the former leper hospital of St Leonard) which had become a charitable institution for the care of old men and young boys. Orford church is depicted with a tower; Sudbourne church's tower has a tall spire (see p. 23 below).

The first true map (as opposed to a chart) of the area was produced in 1600–1602 for Sir Michael Stanhope. He was a courtier to Queen Elizabeth I and to King James I, and he had purchased the manor of Sudbourne from the Crown. John Norden, an

2   Thorpe was Aldeburgh's harbour: H. P. Clodd, *Aldeburgh, the History of an Ancient Borough*, Norman Adlard, 1959, pp. 9, 10; Norman Scarfe, *The Suffolk Landscape*, Phillimore, new edn 2002, p. 168.
3   Judith Middleton-Stewart, 'Down to the sea in ships: decline and fall on the Suffolk coast', *Counties and Communities, Essays on East Anglian History presented to Hassell Smith*, Centre of East Anglian Studies, University of East Anglia, 1996, p. 69.
4   *Victoria County History of Suffolk*, Volume II, p. 13, referring to the Norwich Taxation of 1256 and Joanna Martin, 'Ecclesiastical Jurisdictions', *An Historical Atlas of Suffolk* (edited by David Dymond and Edward Martin), Suffolk County Council, 3rd edn, rev. and enlarged 1999, p. 25. The parish of Orford and Sudbourne is now in a newly formed Woodbridge Deanery.
5   In his will, dated 1426, John Osborn, rector of 'the parish church of Sudbourne with the chapel of Orford annexed', asked that he be buried in the middle of the choir of Orford church. He gave 'to the reparation of the same chancel £10 and to the reparation of the rectory there £5'. He also gave money towards the building of the south porch at Sudbourne church (Norwich Consistory Court wills, 146 Hyrmyng).
6   British Library, MSS Cotton, Aug. 1. 1. 64.

expert cartographer, made a series of detailed maps of the whole estate.[7] He depicts 'Chapmans or Sudburn howse' as a typical manor-house complex. A gabled brick house is surrounded by outbuildings and barns, some round a courtyard. This is more than a working farm, however. The grounds have been laid out as a formal garden and the whole is enclosed by a substantial fence or wall with gates in it. The caption to that sheet of the map gives a description of Sir Michael Stanhope's improvements:

> In this table is contained part of the Manor of Orford, part of Gedgrave, part of Chillesford park, part of Sudbourne, together with Sudbourne house sometimes called Chapmans. Now neatly beautified and adorned with pleasant and delightful walks and shadowing trees. And plentifully stored with variety of all kind of plants of the rarest fruits; apples, pears, plums, apricots and cherries. With other things delightful and profitable, fish and fowl, were the ponds and fleet accordingly respected and used, the woods and groves seen unto and the hawkers, hunters, snarers, and gunners banished, without which you shall be deprived both of your pleasure and profit.[8]

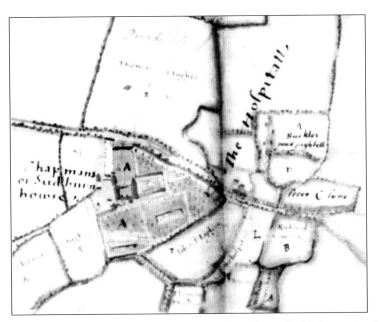

Sir Michael Stanhope's house 'Chapmans or Sudburn howse' with its newly planted gardens: enlarged detail of Map xv of John Norden's survey *c.* 1601

7   Suffolk Record Office (Ipswich) EE5/11/1.
8   Ibid., Map xv.

The only possible blot on this splendid landscape (apart from the troublesome sportsmen) was the hospital. It would have consisted of a number of buildings including a chapel and a house for the master as well as accommodation for the brethren, as the inmates were called. This little settlement can be seen on the map, crowded up close to the fence around the grounds of the hall. It seems that around 1603 Sir Michael Stanhope closed down the hospital. It is believed that the origin of an annual payment or rentcharge of £30, made to the New Orford Town Trust to this day by the owner of what is left of the Sudbourne estate, was to enable the corporation to make alternative provision for the needy men and boys of the town.[9]

Thus the 'gentrification' of Sudbourne Hall was complete and for the next three hundred and fifty years it was the centre of a large and flourishing estate.

It is not clear which of the two churches of Orford and Sudbourne was regarded as the estate church. What information we can glean is of a relatively late date and seems to show that in fact both churches had that function.

Sir Michael Stanhope's sumptuous tomb is in Sudbourne church, as are the hatchments[10] of later owners of the Sudbourne estate, four members of the Devereux family and the 2nd and 3rd Marquises of Hertford. However, when David Elisha Davy first visited Orford church in 1808 he recorded a Devereux hatchment of 1700 at Orford. On his visit in 1842 shortly after the death of the 3rd Marquis of Hertford he noted that 'the pulpit is hung with black cloth & in the front of it is an escutcheon of his arms'.[11] It seems, therefore, that those two hatchments were moved to Sudbourne church at a later date.

The Orford churchwardens' account books of the eighteenth and nineteenth centuries show that as well as paying substantial church rates, the Marquises of Hertford and Sir Richard Wallace made regular additional contributions to Orford church funds.[12]

A plan of Orford church made by Davy in 1832 does not identify a Hertford pew. It is only on a plan made in the 1890s just before the Revd Edward Scott's major restoration[13] that the north-east chapel is marked as the Hertford pew. When Sir

9 *Report of the Commissions for Inquiry Concerning Charities*, ordered to be printed 1829, entry on Orford, Suffolk, p. 566, and Jane Allen, 'The search for the hospital of St Leonard', *Orford & District Local History Bulletin*, Issue 6, 2006, p. 9.

10 Diamond-shaped boards painted with a coat of arms, carried in the funeral procession of the holder of the arms and often subsequently displayed in the estate church.

11 *Collection for the History of Suffolk by Hundreds and Parishes*, British Library Add MSS 19077–19113 (microfilm in SRO (I)).

12 SRO (I) FC168/E5/1, FC168/E5/2.

13 *Plan of Orford church showing the original position of the brasses, c. 1890* by William Sancroft Randall, hanging in St Bartholomew's church on west wall of south aisle.

Effigy of Sir Michael Stanhope on his monument in Sudbourne church

Hatchments in Sudbourne church

Richard Wallace restored Sudbourne church in 1879 a family pew was created in a newly built shallow south transept and lined with handsome wainscotting which was almost certainly a re-use of earlier panelling which could have formed part of an eighteenth-century altarpiece.[14]

The evidence of Kenneth Clark (later Lord Clark, the distinguished art expert and Director of the National Gallery) who spent a lonely, but, he insists, happy, childhood at Sudbourne Hall, is amusing but inconclusive. His father was a Scottish millionaire, who owned the Sudbourne estate from 1903 until the end of the First World War. Kenneth Clark wrote in his autobiography:

Of conventional religious instruction I received nothing at all. My father's mother [who lived in Castle House in Orford] had been in the habit of saying about church-going 'if it doesn't do you any good, it can't do you any harm', and on the strength of this somewhat negative judgement I was sent to Sudbourne Church on Sunday. My mother felt it was her duty to go once or twice, but she

14 D. P. Mortlock, *The Popular Guide to Suffolk Churches No. 3 East Suffolk*, Acorn Editions, 1992, p. 192.

hated church with real animosity . . . My father went once out of bravado. Sudbourne church is small, my father was large and conspicuous and, as he entered the nave, it seemed as if the ship of Christ would founder. The organist dropped his music, the choirboys stopped singing, and the parson fumbled with his words. After a few minutes my father stalked out, bored and disgusted, and trotted off home . . . My own church going was gradually reduced . . .[15]

But in another memoir which he contributed to a book published as a tribute to the composer Benjamin Britten, he wrote:

To sit in Orford church, where I had spent so many hours of my childhood duti-fully awaiting some spark of divine fire, and to receive it at last in the perfor-mance of *Noye's Fludde* [the first performance was given in Orford church in 1958], was an overwhelming experience.[16]

Perhaps the honours should be divided equally between the two churches.

In spite of its distance from the homes of the members of its congregation, All Saints', Sudbourne remains a well-loved, well-attended and beautifully cared-for village church.

Sudbourne Hall was rebuilt in the late eighteenth century (see p. 23 below) and was greatly embellished by Sir Richard Wallace and later owners in the Edwardian era. A new kitchen wing was added as late as the 1920s. Thereafter it suffered the fate of many of the large country houses of England. After an enforced sale in the Depres-sion of the 1930s it was unoccupied until it was requisitioned by the army during the Second World War. When the war ended the house was returned to its owner, Sir Peter Greenwell, but it was in such poor condition that the main portion was demolished in 1951. In the 1980s the buildings that remained, including the stable yard, the game larder, laundry and kitchen, were converted into houses and there is once again a flourishing community at Sudbourne Hall.

15 Kenneth Clark, *Another Part of the Wood*, John Murray, 1974, p. 11.
16 Kenneth Clark, 'The Other Side of the Alde' in *Tribute to Benjamin Britten on his Fiftieth Birthday*, edited by Anthony Gishford, Faber and Faber, 1963, p. 44, and see pp. 72 and 73, below.

2

A Brief History of the Structure of Orford Church

St Bartholomew's church in Orford has been subject to works of one sort or another in almost every century of its existence.

The original huge Norman church, probably built soon after, or perhaps at the same time as, the castle (1165–73), was drastically altered in *c.* 1320–40 when the nave and aisles were rebuilt, the central tower removed and a new tower built at the west end. Thereafter for nearly four hundred years the church consisted of a tower, lofty nave and aisles (the south aisle being unusually wide, almost the same width as the nave) and the (slightly lower) Norman chancel. The chancel had a stone vault[1] and architectural detail of the highest quality, some of which can still be seen – an arcade with gallery above and the piers embellished in relief rather than the more usual incised decoration (see the photographs on pp. 19 and 119).[2]

The font dates from the fifteenth century[3] when the porch was added and the Norman chancel altered and truncated.[4] A rood loft was built with access up a stair cut into one of the remaining Norman crossing piers. Side altars, in chapels screened off from the body of the nave, were set up. In the north-east corner near the rood stair there was a niche for a statue in one of the former transept arches and the image of the Virgin Mary placed there was known as Our Lady in the Wall. Altars, chapels and images of St Nicholas, Our Lady of Pity, St Bartholomew, St Christopher, St John the Baptist and St Anne were all to be found in the church. Bequests were made to embellish and repair them right up to the time of the Reformation. A number of

1   Lawrence R. Hoey and Malcolm Thurlby, 'A survey of Romanesque vaulting in Great Britain and Ireland', *Antiquaries Journal*, vol. 84, 2004, pp. 117–84 (although the authors' statement on p. 119 that Orford was a collegiate church, i.e. a church endowed for a college or chapter of priests, is without foundation).

2   These 'sophisticated and evocative ruins' and many other features of the church are described by Norman Scarfe in an article on St Bartholomew's, Orford, specially written for the programme of two concerts held in the church on 29 and 30 August 2003, organized by Music in Country Churches.

3   The inscription, in Latin, reads 'Pray for the souls of John Cokerell and his wife Katherine who had this font made to the honour of God'. Katherine Cockerell (the daughter of Thomas de Ickworth) died in 1428.

4   Archaeological excavations were carried out by F. H. Fairweather in 1930 and reported in the *Antiquaries Journal*. The article is reproduced as Appendix II in R. A. Roberts (The Rector's Warden), *'Oreford-Nigh-the-Seas'*, Richard Clay, Bungay, 1935, p. 63.

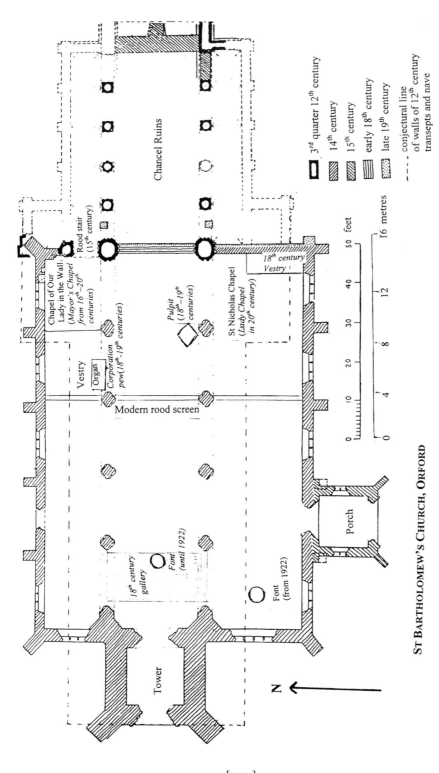

St Bartholomew's Church, Orford

Orford church based on the plan made at the time of the archaeological investigations in 1930 and showing features (*identified in italics*) marked on David Elisha Davy's plan of *c.* 1820

Chancel Ruins

Rood stair (15th century)

Chapel of Our Lady in the Wall (*Mayor's Chapel from 16th–20th centuries*)

Vestry

Organ

Corporation pew (18th–19th centuries)

Modern rood screen

Pulpit (18th–19th centuries)

St Nicholas Chapel (*Lady Chapel in 20th century*)

18th century Vestry

18th century gallery

Font (until 1922)

Font (from 1922)

Porch

Tower

N

3rd quarter 12th century
14th century
15th century
early 18th century
late 19th century
conjectural line of walls of 12th century transepts and nave

50 feet
16 metres

0 10 20 30 40 50

0 4 8 12 16

brasses on the floor at the east end of the church almost certainly depict some of those pious testators, although the inscriptions which once identified them have gone.[5]

We do not know what happened to the fabric of the church in the reigns of King Edward VI (1547–53) and Queen Mary (1553–58). A pew in the south aisle was designated for the use of the people of the hamlet of Gedgrave (just one mile to the west of Orford) after their parish church, of which no trace remains, was closed and the living annexed to that of Orford in 1557.[6] Early in the reign of Queen Elizabeth I Orford church roof was replaced[7] by one with a much lower pitch than the fourteenth-century one and, judging from the glimpse of it in the photograph of the south aisle on p. 57 it was of a fairly 'rustic' quality.

Orford became a chartered borough in 1579 and the Mayor's Chapel was established at the east end of the north aisle, known in pre-Reformation times (and re-dedicated in 2005) as the Chapel of Our Lady in the Wall. There James Coe, the first mayor, was buried in 1591, as were a number of his successors. In 1599 Francis Mason, a noted theologian, became rector. He rebuilt the rectory and wrote learned books in defence of the authority of the Church of England. He died in 1621 and his monument, originally in the Norman chancel, has been moved to the wall of the St Nicholas Chapel in the south-east corner of the church. One of Francis Mason's books, 'A Vindication of the Church of England', first published in Latin, was translated into English and reissued or edited many times, the last version being published in 1768 – an astonishingly long life for a work of theology.[8]

The finest of the Orford brasses, that of Bridget Bence (wife of another mayor, Robert Bence) and her daughter Joan Wheatley, who died in 1605 and 1603 respectively, is on the floor to the north of the St Nicholas Chapel altar. John Coggeshall, three times mayor, was buried in the Mayor's Chapel in 1633, his grave also marked by an interesting brass. New bells were acquired. Those dated 1639, 1649 and two of 1679 have been repaired and are part of the present ring (see p. 128 below). A church-wardens' chest bears the date 1634.

The middle years of the seventeenth century also saw a visit from the puritan iconoclast, William Dowsing. His Journal tells us that on 25 January 1644 at Orford,

---

5   Edmund Farrer, *List of Suffolk Brasses*, 1903, pp. 46–8. A buckle set in the stone by one image of a woman, her three sons and seven daughters, would seem to indicate that she was a member of the Buckle (or Bokyll) family who gave their name to a property on the Market Square next to the site of the present Town Hall, see Vic Harrup, 'The Buckle family of Orford at a time of religious change,' *Orford & District Local History Bulletin*, Issue 7, 2006, p. 11.

6   'Oreford-Nigh-the-Seas', see n. 4, above, pp. 33, 36, 58.

7   Covenant for re-roofing the parish church of Orford, 29 June 1562, SRO(I) EE5/6/65.

8   H. W. B. Wayman, *The Monumental Inscriptions Remaining in the Church of St Bartholomew at Orford in Suffolk*, The English Monumental Inscriptions Society, 1911, pp. 23–7.

We brake down 28 superstitious pictures; and took up 11 popish inscriptions in brass; and gave orders for digging up the steps, and takeing of 2 crosses off the steeple, one off the church, and one off the [chancel], in all four.[9]

He also went to Snape and Sternfield that day. The following day it was Sudbourne's turn where, 'We brake down 6 pictures; and gave order for the taking down a cross on the steeple; and the steps to be levelled.'[10]

The latter part of the century seems to have been a low point at Orford. An archdeacon's visitation in 1686 found, *inter alia*, 'leads decayed; rain in several places. Floor of south aisle sunk. Great bell split. Partition of church and chancel decayed.'[11]

Help arrived in the person of the Revd Josiah Alsop who became rector in 1700 and who seems to have been just as energetic as the Revd Edward Scott nearly two hundred years later.

The remarkable concentration of Parliamentary seats on the Suffolk coast (two each for Dunwich, Aldeburgh and Orford) combined with economic decline, made the area a magnet for the attentions of absentee grandees. In Orford's case Sir Edward Turner (or Turnour), had a lease on the two lighthouses on Orford Ness which brought him the lucrative tolls paid by passing shipping. He was one of the two Members of Parliament from 1701 to 1709 and then from 1710 until his death in 1721. The benefaction boards (now on the north wall of the church) show that Josiah Alsop extracted substantial sums from Sir Edward Turner, his local agent John Hook and others, including the twelve freemen of the borough (who were the voters), so that he could undertake his plan to modernize the church. The Norman chancel was abandoned and a new east wall was built. The interior was completely refitted. There was a new communion table surrounded by a rail. A hexagonal pulpit with a canopy or sounding board was placed against the most easterly free-standing pillar on the south side. There were new pews, including a handsome pew for the mayor and corporation between the first and second pillars on the north side. (Judging from Emmeline Rope's painting, p. 63, below, that pew possibly also incorporated a clerk's or reader's desk). Behind the altar were boards painted with the Ten Commandments, flanked by the paintings of Moses and Aaron which now hang at the west end of the church. On either side of the paintings were boards with the Lord's Prayer and Creed. Equally prominent, and flanking the east window, were the benefaction boards, so the parishioners were left in no doubt as to who had paid for what.

The church then must in many ways have looked remarkably like the fashionable

---

9 Trevor Cooper (ed.), *The Journal of William Dowsing*, Ecclesiological Society and The Boydell Press, 2001, p. 221.

10 Ibid., p. 224.

11 *'Oreford Nigh-the-Seas'*, p. 33.

new churches and chapels being built at that time (remember that the rood screen which now divides the church was not there). This was the look to which the parishioners aspired. When they petitioned the bishop in 1708 asking to demolish the chancel, one of the reasons they gave for wanting to do the work was

> a low Chancel at ye end of a church is no where found but in ye old Gothick parish churches, for all ye Modern Churches of London, Holland and other parts of Europe, both papist and Protestant are all of ye same height from end to end without any low projection for a Chancell, as are ye 2 best churches in Xtiendom, St Paul's in London, and St Peter's in Rome.[12]

It is rather surprising that at that time a Church of England congregation in rural Suffolk was prepared to cite the example of the 'papist' St Peter's in Rome in support of their petition to the bishop.

The eighteenth-century churchwardens' accounts show a steady programme of maintenance, if not restoration, work. It is known that for at least part of the eighteenth century a school was held in the south porch, where the teacher was the father of the poet, George Crabbe.[13] In 1772 the Earl of Hertford (who had acquired the Sudbourne estate) gave an organ which was erected on a free-standing gallery in front of the tower arch. The £2 cost of the gilded inscribed board recording the gift was, however, borne by the church,[14] which might explain why it has survived to this day, now forming part of the partition between the vestry and the Chapel of Our Lady in the Wall. The Earl also gave some silver communion plate (see pp. 21, 23 and 64, below).

David Elisha Davy, the antiquary, who visited and made notes at Orford four times between 1808 and 1842, gives a very clear description of the church at that time (including a plan). He did not seem to have found the church in a bad state, apart from the tower which fell in 1830. The petition sent by the parish requesting funds for repairs after that disaster did, however, describe the church as being 'in a dilapidated state as to the walls and roof' (see p. 124, below). When recording his visit in 1832 Davey noted the new memorial tablet (above the north door) to the Revd John Connor, the Irish parson who had served as curate for forty-one years and as rector for just twenty-one months before he died in September 1830 at the age of seventy-three. Davy could not resist adding the gossipy snippet,

---

12 L. Dow, 'Orford Church in 1706', *Proceedings of the Suffolk Institute of Archaeology*, vol. 26 (1952–54), p. 225.

13 Revd George Crabbe, *Crabbe's Life and Poems*, 1834, vol. 1, p. 4. The poet Crabbe was born in Aldeburgh. One of his poems, *The Borough*, contains the story of Peter Grimes, which formed the basis of the libretto of Benjamin Britten's opera, first performed in 1945.

14 Churchwardens' Book 1744–89 (disbursements 1772–73), SRO (I), EC168/E5/1.

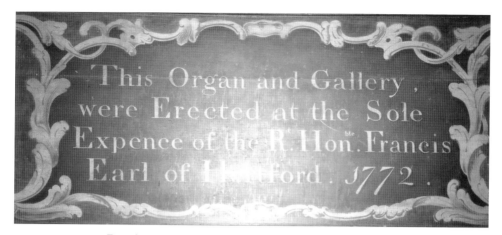

Board recording the gift of the organ and gallery in 1772

Mr Connor is said to have been a natural son of Francis 1st Marquis of Hertford, he was certainly always patronised by the family at Sudbourne, though it
was very late in life before he obtained any preferment [i.e. a living of his own]
from them in England.[15]

John Connor did indeed come from Lisburn, County Antrim, where the Hertford
family had an estate. If he was a son of the 1st Marquis, then he would have been the
second to serve as rector. From 1781 to 1784 the Hon. Edward Seymour Conway, the
fourth (legitimate) son of the 1st Marquis held the living, but he died at the early age
of thirty-two at Lyons in France.[16]

The 'restoration story' at Orford usually starts with the statement in the 1874
edition of *White's Directory and History of Suffolk* that there was restoration work in
the nave, including the windows, in 1853. The churchwardens' books of disbursements are unfortunately missing for the period from 1786 to 1866 and when application was made to the Incorporated Church Building Society for funds in 1894, the
question on the form asking for details of when repairs were last done was not
answered.

We do know that some pews were put in the south aisle between 1842 and 1877 by
the rector, the Revd John Maynard (see chapter 11, below), and it seems likely that he
may have been responsible for other work there. Davy's plan of 1832 shows the south
east end of the church partitioned off to form a vestry where the St Nicholas chapel

15 British Library Add. MSS 19077-19181 (microfilm in SRO (I)).
16 *'Oreford-Nigh-the-Seas'*, p. 62.

Revd John Maynard, *c*.1870

altar is today. A letter written in 1894 at the beginning of the Revd Edward Scott's restoration campaign (see p. 61, below) refers to the south aisle 'as now "restored"', which could well mean more than its adaptation to serve as the main place of worship while work was being undertaken in the nave and north aisle. The interesting photograph of the south aisle at that time shows some enormous heating pipes at the back of the pews and beside the chairs. The Revd John Maynard's memorial wall brass can be seen on the east wall to the left of the altar (see p. 57, below). This location may have been because he had made changes in that part of the church.

The memorial, which has been moved to the north wall of the church, reads:

To the glory of God and in loving memory of John Maynard MA for 35 years rector of Sudbourne cum Orford who died Septr. 13 1877 aged 79 years. Also of his son Walter Fawkes Maynard MA for 10 years curate of the same parishes who died Novr. 29 1874 aged 43 years. Also of Walter Edwin Maynard BA son of Walter Fawkes Maynard who died at Jabalpur India August 2nd 1887 aged 21 years. So He giveth His beloved Sleep.

The Revd John Maynard was born on the island of Nevis in the West Indies, where his family owned a plantation. He obtained his degree at Exeter College, Oxford and started his clerical career in Gloucestershire. He and his wife Elizabeth were beset by tragedy. Their first son, John, died when still at school. In October 1871 his surviving son and curate, Walter, was sent from Orford to the West Indies with his wife and four young children for a year in the hope that he would be cured of the tuberculosis from which he was by then suffering. Walter did live for two more years after his return and he and his wife Louisa had another daughter, but the baby died soon after her father. Elizabeth, John Maynard's daughter, married a clergyman friend of her brother's, the Revd Charles Raymond (see p. 44 below), but she, too, died of tuberculosis, leaving three young children.

Walter Edwin Maynard, John Maynard's grandson, also commemorated on the memorial plaque, and who had been a popular sportsman at Oxford, where he coxed his college boat, died of typhoid when visiting another of his relatives in India.[17]

The connection with Orford of the surviving members of the Maynard family, however, lasted for well over one hundred years (see pp. 4 above and 128 below). Many Maynards are buried in the churchyard; their graves are in the ruined Norman chancel.

Maynard family graves in the Norman chancel

17 Information about the Maynard family from Bessie Scott's memoir, see p. 41 below and details of John Maynard's clerical career from *Crockford's Clerical Directory* of 1877, which also states that he was 'Chaplain to the Marquis of Hertford'.

The Orford church terriers (inventories of land, buildings and goods) from 1845 to 1922, encompassing the whole period being examined in this book, have survived. They, as well as the inscriptions on some of the furnishings marking the munificence of almost every member of the Scott family, enable us to date the arrival, and identify the donors, of most of the contents of the church.

Before the Scott era, the 1845 and 1865 terriers, and those of 1872 and 1879 (which are slightly less detailed), list:

An elegant organ the gift of the Marquis of Hertford in the year 1772. Item the number of bells are five and one day clock. The communion plate is 1st A large chased silver flagon and cover holding about two quarts marked I H S. 2nd A chased cup holding about a pint and a half marked in the same way. 3rd A salver with a chased rim supported with three globular legs. 4th A small ditto upper rim plain under rim and bottom rim chased all of them the gift of the Marquis of Hertford whose name is engraved upon them likewise a silver bason for collecting the alms. Given to the parish by Wilhelmine widow of Alfred Fawkes Esquire.[18] Item the furniture of the pulpit and desk is of scarlet cloth with silk fringe. That of the communion table crimson velvet with the letters I H S and fringe of gold lace and also a fine white linen cloth and napkin for the Communion Service.

The church still possesses some of the communion plate (see p. 64 below), but the salver with globular legs and the 'silver bason' have, unfortunately, disappeared.

A water colour by Emmeline Rope dated 1885 (see p. 63 below) shows how the east end of the nave retained its eighteenth-century appearance almost to the end of the nineteenth century. There are bands of black paint around the tops of the pillars, explained in the caption to the picture as 'mourning for the death of king George IV'. That generally unlamented monarch died in 1830, so the special relationship that he had with the Marquises of Hertford (see chapter 3, below) was commemorated in Orford church for a very long time.

---

18 The coincidence of the name Fawkes with that of Walter Fawkes Maynard would indicate a connection, but I have been unable to establish what it was. The 1851 and 1861 censuses tell us that the widowed Mrs Wilhelmina Fawkes was then living in London.

3

The Marquises of Hertford and Richard Wallace

In 1754 Francis Seymour Conway, Earl of Hertford, who became the first Marquis of Hertford in 1793, acquired the Sudbourne estate (which included most of the property in Orford). He purchased it from the executors of Price Devereux, the 10th Viscount Hereford, whose ancestor, Leicester Devereux, the 6th Viscount, had married a granddaughter of Sir Michael Stanhope (see p. 7 above).[1] The estate remained in the family of the Marquises of Hertford for a hundred and thirty years until Sir Richard Wallace sold it in 1884.

The family was descended from Edward Seymour (*c.*1506–1552), the Protector, Duke of Somerset and Earl of Hertford, whose sister Jane was Henry VIII's third wife and the mother of King Edward VI.

By the eighteenth century the Hertfords were Tory grandees, exercising power through their intelligence, wealth, the number of parliamentary seats that they could control and friendship with the royal family. Their main residence was, and still is, Ragley Hall in Warwickshire. The 1st Marquis also had estates in Ireland and Cornwall. He served successively as ambassador to France, Lord Lieutenant of Ireland and Lord Chamberlain. Around 1784 he had Sudbourne Hall rebuilt to a fairly austere design by the architect James Wyatt. *The Suffolk Traveller* of 1829 describes it as 'a plain quadrangular building . . . covered with a white composition, and the staircase is executed with [Wyatt's] usual skill and taste, the whole conveying an idea of simplicity rather than elegance. It has been chiefly used as a sporting residence.' It must have presented a startling contrast to Sir Michael Stanhope's jettied and rambling 'Sudburn howse' shown on the map on p. 8 above and the Elizabethan coastal chart.

As we have seen, the Earl donated items to Orford church. The silver communion plate which he presented is engraved: 'Given by the Earl of Hertford to the united parishes of Sudbourn and Orford', and is of considerable interest. It was made in Birmingham (about twenty miles from Ragley Hall) by Matthew Boulton[2] and John

---

1 W. A. Copinger, *Manors of Suffolk*, Manchester, 1905–11, vol. v, p. 177.
2 Matthew Boulton (1728–1809) was a craftsman, scientist, thinker, industrialist and entrepreneur. Initially he was in business making metal articles at his Soho manufactory near Birmingham (in partnership with John Fothergill), but in 1775 he went into partnership with James Watt to manufacture steam engines which powered the Industrial Revolution both in Great Britain and throughout the world.

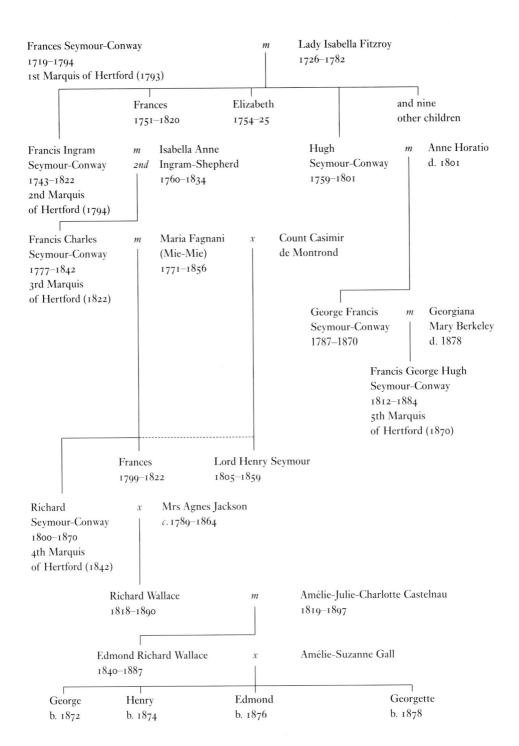

Frances Seymour-Conway
1719–1794
1st Marquis of Hertford (1793)

m

Lady Isabella Fitzroy
1726–1782

Frances
1751–1820

Elizabeth
1754–25

and nine
other children

Francis Ingram
Seymour-Conway
1743–1822
2nd Marquis
of Hertford (1794)

m
2nd

Isabella Anne
Ingram-Shepherd
1760–1834

Hugh
Seymour-Conway
1759–1801

m

Anne Horatio
d. 1801

Francis Charles
Seymour-Conway
1777–1842
3rd Marquis
of Hertford (1822)

m

Maria Fagnani
(Mie-Mie)
1771–1856

x

Count Casimir
de Montrond

George Francis
Seymour-Conway
1787–1870

m

Georgiana
Mary Berkeley
d. 1878

Francis George Hugh
Seymour-Conway
1812–1884
5th Marquis
of Hertford (1870)

Frances
1799–1822

Lord Henry Seymour
1805–1859

Richard
Seymour-Conway
1800–1870
4th Marquis
of Hertford (1842)

x

Mrs Agnes Jackson
*c.*1789–1864

Richard Wallace
1818–1890

m

Amélie-Julie-Charlotte Castelnau
1819–1897

Edmond Richard Wallace
1840–1887

x

Amélie-Suzanne Gall

George
b. 1872

Henry
b. 1874

Edmond
b. 1876

Georgette
b. 1878

Hertford and Wallace family tree

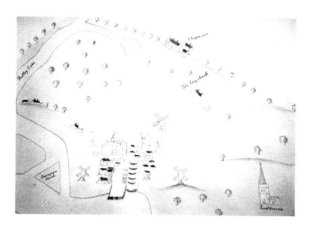

From 'Chapmans' to Sudbourne Hall: *top* a detail from the coastal chart *c.* 1570–80; *below* the rebuilt Sudbourne Hall, engraving *c.* 1800

Fothergill and bears the date mark of the very first year of the Birmingham assay office, 1773. The Earl's generosity towards his Suffolk estate's parish church was not, however, unbounded. The Boulton & Fothergill order books record that the flagon and chalice, priced together at £35 4s 1d, were sent in February 1774 and had been made as 'light as the nature of the work would possibly admit', in order to keep the cost down.[3] They may now be seen in the Gallery of Sacred Silver and Stained Glass at the Victoria and Albert Museum, where they are on long-term loan.

The 2nd Marquis, like his father, followed a diplomatic career and continued the close association with the royal household, serving as Lord Chamberlain from 1812 to 1821. In 1794 he inherited the title and he acquired a house in Manchester Square as his

3   Matthew Boulton Papers, Letter Book, [B&F] to Earl of Hertford, 26 February 1774, Birmingham City Archives MS 3782/1/38. Information supplied by Ann Eatwell of the Victoria and Albert Museum and Birmingham City Archives.

London residence. His wife, the 2nd Marchioness, was a friend and confidante of the Prince Regent for more than a decade until he came to the throne as King George IV in 1820. (Incidentally, whilst the friendship lasted, she turned the Prince away from the Whigs, the party with whom, for most of his life, he was associated). It was probably the 2nd Marquis who was responsible for the Georgian appearance of so many of the houses in Orford. Brick fronts, new windows and elegant doorcases were put on to many of the sixteenth- and seventeenth-century timber-framed houses, giving the old streets of the village their pleasingly uniform character.

The enclosure of Sudbourne Common by Act of Parliament in 1807 and its division between the proprietors (the lion's share going to the 2nd Marquis), led to the development of what is now the main settlement of Sudbourne village.[4]

The 3rd Marquis had twenty-four years in the House of Commons before he succeeded his father in June 1822. One of the seats he held for a time was Orford. It is likely that the Orford Parliamentary seats were an important factor in his grandfather, the Earl of Hertford's, decision to purchase the Sudbourne estate, a habit which was not lost in succeeding generations. Thomas Creevey commented, when the 3rd Marquis was created a Knight of the Garter in November 1822, 'Lord Hertford owes his blue ribbon to his having purchased *four* seats in Parliament since his father's death, and to his avowed intention of dealing still more largely in the same commodity . . .'[5]

This state of affairs was not to last much longer. The Reform Act of 1832 swept away many of the 'rotten boroughs' and Creevey gleefully wrote: 'Well, our Reform rises in publick affection every instant . . . To think of dear Aldborough and Orford, both belonging to Lord Hertford, and purchased at great price, being clearly bowled out, without a word of with your leave or by your leave.' (Here Creevey is referring to Aldeburgh in Suffolk. Rather confusingly, Aldborough in Yorkshire was also a pocket borough, but it was in the hands of the Duke of Newcastle. Creevey calls them 'both the rottenest of the rotten'.) Amongst others, the Hertfords also controlled the boroughs of Camelford in Cornwall and Lisburn in County Antrim.[6]

In spite of the disappearance of the Parliamentary seats the Sudbourne estate did not lose its attraction. It had become a fine sporting estate and provided some of the best shooting in the country. The Earl of Hertford had been responsible for introducing the French or red-legged partridge to England in 1770 when he brought the birds over from France to Sudbourne. Since then they have spread all over the

4 Tom Williamson, *Sandlands: The Suffolk Coast and Heaths*, Windgather Press, 2005, p. 80.
5 *The Creevey Papers* (edited by Sir Herbert Maxwell), John Murray, 1903, vol. II, p. 56. Creevey was a Whig MP, so he was by no means an impartial commentator on the activities of Lord Hertford.
6 Ibid., pp. 221 and 227. See also, John Ingamells, *The 3rd Marquess of Hertford as a Collector*, Wallace Collection, 1983, p. 12.

country.[7] The Prince Regent and the Duke of Wellington were both regular guests of the 2nd Marquis. The Prince was staying at Sudbourne in November 1817 when he was brought the news that his popular and adored only daughter, Princess Charlotte, had gone into labour and that it was going badly. His coach drove through the night back to London. By the time he arrived the Princess had been delivered of a still-born baby boy and a few hours later she, too, was dead.[8]

As we have seen, the 3rd Marquis took a very active role in politics. His private life was notorious, and he became increasingly debauched as he grew older. Lord Steyne in Thackeray's novel *Vanity Fair* which appeared in 1847–48, after the 3rd Marquis's death in 1842, is believed to be based on him.[9]

An altogether kinder picture of the 3rd Marquis emerges in the pages of *Harriette Wilson's Memoirs*. Harriette, a good-time girl of the Regency period, published her memoirs in 1825. Harriette's sister, Fanny, had been a mistress of Lord Hertford. When Fanny became terminally ill, Harriette reports that she met the Marquis as he ran downstairs from Fanny's room on his way to fetch a surgeon to attend her. He arranged for straw to be put down by her door (in order to soften the sound of the passing traffic) and paid her 'constant, steady attentions'. He sat with her when she was dying:

> Fanny was not able to talk much; but she seemed gratified and happy to see him. When His Lordship was about to depart, she held out her hand to him. Hertford said, in a tone of much real feeling, 'God bless you, poor thing', and then left the room.[10]

In his will the 3rd Marquis left the sum of £100 to the poor of Orford. This was probably a conventional gesture from the local landowner, but the account of the distribution shows how his legacy must have made a real difference to quite a number of needy individuals.[11] Twenty-four payments of sums between ten shillings and three shillings and sixpence were made, and five payments of poor rates from £1 16s 5d to one shilling. Seventeen payments were made to six different shoemakers for the supply of shoes totalling £23 6s 10d, then:

7 James Wentworth Day 'Comment', *East Anglian Magazine*, vol. 25, no. 12, October 1966, p. 402.
8 Christopher Hibbert, *George IV*, Allen Lane, 1975, p. 99. This double tragedy meant that George IV had no descendants. The throne eventually went to his brother who became King William IV and, as he, too, was childless, the next in line was their niece, who in 1837 became the young Queen Victoria.
9 William Makepeace Thackeray, *Vanity Fair*, 1847–48, chapter 64. The last paragraph of the chapter describes how, after Lord Steyne's death, 'his will was a good deal disputed', thus providing a fictional foretaste of the real events recounted in chapter 14 of this book.
10 *Harriette Wilson's Memoirs* (1825), reprinted by Peter Davies, 1929, p. 630.
11 Account of distribution of Lord Hertford's legacy to the poor, 5 March 1843, SRO (I), FC168/A3/2.

In small sums to Sudbourne people 12s

£1.9.6 for meat for sundry poor

Paid for apparel and goods Mr Rope[12] £16.15.2

Mr Mingay[13] for coals 5s

Mr Kindred at Christmas for meat £2.0.0

Mr Peck for Sunday School books £2.12.0

Mr Turner for Sunday School books 6s.1d.

When a young man of twenty-one, the 3rd Marquis had married Maria Fagnani (Mie-Mie), the illegitimate daughter of an Italian dancer and the 4th Duke of Queensberry.[14] The Duke and another rich man, George Selwyn, both believed themselves to be Mie-Mie's father, so both left her large amounts of money in their wills. Queensberry also left money to those two of Mie-Mie's children who did not inherit the Hertford title, a girl and a boy, the 4th Marquis's sister, Frances, and half-brother, Lord Henry Seymour (see the family tree, p. 22 above).

From 1802, after only four years of marriage, the 3rd Marchioness lived apart from her husband in Paris with her children. Her elder son, who eventually became the 4th Marquis, was thus brought up in France and indeed spent scarcely more than ten years of his life in England and Ireland.

Unlike his father, grandfather and great-grandfather, the 4th Marquis took no part in public affairs. From 1835 he lived mainly in Paris, in considerable splendour, as a recluse. He was unmarried, but in 1818 he had a son, Richard, whose mother was Mrs Agnes Jackson. From the age of six, Richard Jackson was brought up in Paris by his grandmother Mie-Mie (the 3rd Marchioness). He changed his name to his mother's maiden name, Wallace, in 1842, the year his father the 4th Marquis inherited the Hertford title.

Richard Wallace acted as his father's secretary and right-hand man. Wallace's mistress from at least 1840, when their son Edmond was born, was Amélie-Julie-Charlotte Castelnau. She was reputed to have been an assistant in a perfumer's shop. They did not marry until 1871, after the death of the 4th Marquis and shortly before they came to live in London and at Sudbourne Hall.

Wallace had been devoted to his grandmother, who had died on 2 March 1856. Years later, in 1879, when Sudbourne church was restored (largely at his expense), the east window was dedicated to her memory. The window, in startlingly bright colours

12 Probably Samuel Rope (1810–1882), grocer, draper and newsagent: *White's Directory, 1844.*

13 George Mingay, shipowner, who in partnership with George Rope (1814–1912), Samuel's brother, traded as corn and coal merchants from Orford Quay: Margaret Poulter, *The Rope Family of Orford*, Orford Museum, 1998.

14 For an account of her life, see Bernard Falk, *'Old Q's' Daughter*, Hutchinson, 1937.

East window in Sudbourne church commemorating Mie–Mie,
the 3rd Marchioness of Hertford

and of mediocre artistry, is the work of Alexander Gibbs (who produced much better work for the architect William Butterfield, which can be seen in All Saints, Margaret Street, London and in Keble College, Oxford[15]). It commemorates the woman whose money helped the acquisition of one of the most exquisite collections of furniture, porcelain and pictures in the world.

The 3rd Marquis, influenced, no doubt, by his friend the Prince Regent who had been a great collector, bought some fine furniture, paintings and *objets d'art*.

It was the 4th Marquis, helped by his large inheritances from both his parents (his *annual* income in 1842 was estimated at £250,000 – a staggering £12,382,500 in

15 D. P. Mortlock, *The Popular Guide to Suffolk Churches No. 3 East Suffolk*, Acorn Editions, 1992, p. 192.

today's money[16]), who was the really serious collector of works of art. He was extremely knowledgeable and had excellent taste, but the cream of his collection, including that part which was later to constitute the Wallace Collection in London, remained for the time being in France. When it came to the acquisition of pictures suitable for Sudbourne Hall, it was a case of 'horses for courses'. He wrote to Samuel Mawson, the man who sometimes acted as his agent in the salerooms, describing some recent purchases which included 'a little rubbish for the country . . . beautiful of the sort & perfect for my shooting place'.[17]

Lord Henry Seymour (born in 1805, the child of the 3rd Marchioness and Count Casimir de Montrond), to whom both Richard Wallace and his father were devoted, died in 1859. He, too, had been a collector and he left the share of his mother's fortune which he had inherited and *objets d'art* to his half-brother, the 4th Marquis. All three men are buried in the Père-Lachaise cemetery in Paris. The vault where they lie is in a large and gloomy funerary chapel in the 28th section of the cemetery.

The Hertford ownership of the Sudbourne estate had a profound effect on Orford. The corporation, which had proudly won independence from the manor when it acquired its charter of incorporation in 1579, became the creature of the estate and its powerful owners. Originally membership of the corporation (and the holding of the offices of mayor, portman, capital burgess, deputy recorder, town clerk and sergeant-at-mace) was only possible for freemen who were inhabitants of the borough. From the late seventeenth century, the practice of electing non-residents as freemen as an honour or in return for the payment of a fee became commonplace. As time went on the selection of those who were admitted as freemen was being made by the estate landowner. An examination of the town records shows that between 1766 and 1872 the corporation consisted on the one hand of the non-resident relatives and friends of the Marquises of Hertford, whilst on the other, the resident members, who were the ones who conducted the business of the borough, were farmers and tradesmen (for the most part also tenants of the estate), employees of the family, and the rector (who also served as chaplain to the current Marquis). During that period of some hundred and ten years years, no fewer than twenty-seven men named Seymour were members of the corporation, serving terms that ranged from two to sixty-four years. Eight of them served a total of twenty-five years as mayor. Almost every one of the Hertford estate stewards held the office of town clerk and deputy recorder.[18]

The former town, with its port, market and merchant families, fatally weakened by economic decline, had assumed the character of an estate village.

16 *The Hertford Mawson Letters* (ed. John Ingamells) Wallace Collection, 1981, p. 10.
17 Ibid., p. 98 (letter of 28 April 1857).
18 Patricia Harvey Fleming, *Villagers and Strangers, an English Proletarian Village over Four Centuries*, Schenken Publishing Company, 1979, pp. 81–5.

4

John Murray Scott and the Wallace Connection

On his father's death in 1870 Richard Wallace inherited the 4th Marquis's dazzlingly high-quality collections and two properties in Paris – a large apartment in the rue Lafitte and Bagatelle, a beautiful house set in sixty acres in the Bois de Boulogne. He was also left substantial estates in Lisburn, County Antrim[1] and a house at 105 Piccadilly, London. The one thing he could not inherit, because of his illegitimacy, was the title and those properties which were entailed, i.e. that went with the title, which included Sudbourne and the house in Manchester Square. In 1872, Sir Richard Wallace bought the Sudbourne estate and the tail-end of the lease on the Manchester Square property from his father's second cousin and heir, Francis George Hugh Seymour, who had become the 5th Marquis. Sir Richard Wallace continued the collection of works of art and antiques, assisted in his turn by a French-speaking secretary, John Murray Scott. The two men met before Richard Wallace had made his move to England.

John Murray Scott[2] was the eldest son of a doctor, also John Scott, and his wife Alicia Lucy Murray.[3] Dr John Scott practised medicine in Boulogne. There was a large English community in Boulogne in the nineteenth century, big enough to support two Anglican churches and a Methodist church. Many of the expatriates were in self-imposed exile for reasons such as bankruptcy or because they had been involved in duels. It seems that however embarrassed their circumstances, they had the sense to pay their doctor's bills, as Dr John Scott seems to have been prosperous.

---

1   There was some costly litigation over the Irish property between Wallace and the person who thought himself to be the residuary legatee of the 4th Marquis's estate, a distant cousin, Sir George Hamilton Seymour. Much of the information about the Marquises of Hertford and Sir Richard Wallace here and in chapter 3 above, comes from *The Founders of the Wallace Collection* by Peter Hughes, published by the Trustees of the Wallace Collection, 1981, and *The Greatest Collector* by Donald Mallett, published by Macmillan, 1979.
2   In order to distinguish him from his father, John Murray Scott is given his full name. In later chapters he is referred to as Sir John or Seery, the nickname given to him by the Sackvilles (see n. 6 to chapter 10).
3   Alicia was the daughter of George St Vincent Thomas Nelson Murray, the first child of Admiral Sir George Murray whose father had been a close friend of Nelson's and was one of the admirals who fought at the Battle of Cape St Vincent (information from one of the Murray descendants, Mrs J. L. Hargest).

Wallace's father, the 4th Marquis of Hertford, was of course neither financially embarrassed nor on the wrong side of the law. During and immediately after 1848, 'The Year of Revolutions' in Europe, a number of English expatriates, including Mie-Mie, the dowager Marchioness, and her sons and grandson, moved temporarily to Boulogne so that they could, if necessary, make a speedy escape back to England. In 1869 the 4th Marquis was taken ill in Boulogne (in fact he was dying) when he was on his way to England from Paris. While he was receiving treatment from Dr John Scott, Wallace was impressed by the doctor's son. John Murray Scott had been educated at Marlborough College, the Sorbonne in Paris and in Germany. He had also been called to the English bar, but in spite of his extensive education appeared to have been living at home with his parents, without occupation.

Then the Franco-Prussian war broke out. The charmed and indolent lifestyle of the 4th Marquis and his son was abruptly terminated. Just as the siege of Paris was about to begin in 1870, the 4th Marquis died. His funeral cortege could move through the streets of Paris to the Père Lachaise cemetery, where he was to be buried, only with great difficulty because of the barricades.

The contents of Bagatelle, which stood outside the city and in the path of the advancing Prussian troops, were hastily moved to the rue Lafitte. This was a wise move because the French military took over Bagatelle and caused considerable damage. At the rue Lafitte steps were taken to protect the precious objects there, the windows were shuttered and earth placed on the roof in case shells fell on it. During the siege Richard Wallace acquitted himself admirably, organizing relief operations to which he donated large sums of money, but his experiences during that dreadful time and during the Commune the following year made him decide to settle in England. When peace was restored and just before he left Paris he made some major acquisitions for the collection – of arms and armour and medieval and Renaissance objects. He made more very generous charitable donations and as a parting gesture he presented fifty ornate cast-iron drinking fountains to the city; they soon became known as *wallaces*, and some of them survive to this day.[4]

Honours were given to him by the French government and in 1871 he was knighted by Queen Victoria. The twenty-four-year-old John Murray Scott, who had been engaged as Wallace's assistant, was with him throughout the siege and Commune (a very testing and atypical introduction to the job he was to hold for the rest of his life) and also made the move from France to England. The young secretary seems to have made himself invaluable to his employers, especially Lady Wallace.

4 In addition to those remaining in Paris, one has been placed in the forecourt of Hertford House in London (the home of the Wallace Collection) and there are others in Lisburn (J. F. Burns, see n. 8 below).

'Wallace' drinking fountain, Allée des Justes, Paris

She never learned to speak English well and found her new life as a society hostess in England rather trying (see Mrs Bessie Scott's memoir, p. 45 below, and the remark of the 1st Earl of Cranbrook, a guest at a shoot in November 1872: 'The dinner was too good, and required care and firmness. Lady Wallace speaks only French, and I took her in [to dinner], to my dismay, and stumbled through some very bad language'[5]).

After he left France, Wallace's first thought was for his father's collection of art and antiques. He renewed the lease on the house in Manchester Square with the intention of enlarging and adapting it so that he could move the most valuable items in the collection from Paris, which had proved to be a hazardous environment, to the safety of London. He decided to name the property Hertford House in honour of the 4th Marquis, whose collection was to be housed there. This move, which doubtless seemed reasonable and logical to Sir Richard Wallace, infuriated the 5th Marquis because, although the house had sometimes been called Hertford House in the past,

5   Sir Francis Watson, 'The Great Wood Party', *Apollo Magazine*, CXXXI, June 1965, pp. 480–81.

[31]

more often, and certainly in the recent past, it had been known as Manchester House. The new Lord Hertford had just bought himself a home in nearby Connaught Place which he (also reasonably and logically) wished to call Hertford House. Both men stuck to their guns, and for a number of years two properties in the same part of London bore that name.[6]

Sir Richard Wallace was generous in allowing the public to see his fabulous collection. For three years from 1872 to 1875 (when he and Lady Wallace were living at 105 Piccadilly and while the alterations were being made to Hertford House) much of the collection which had been brought from Paris was on display in the Bethnal Green Museum, in the poorest part of the East End of London. Later he made other loans, most notably to an Old Masters Exhibition at the Royal Academy in 1888. In this Wallace was following the example of his father, the 4th Marquis, who had loaned 44 pictures to the Manchester Art Treasures Exhibition in 1857, although the loan had caused him great anxiety.[7] Then in 1865 he had allowed 380 items from his collection (mainly armour, furniture and decorative objects) to be exhibited in Paris at an exhibition called the *Musée Retrospectif*.

The life of a landed English gentleman seemed to appeal to Sir Richard Wallace. He took a keen interest in his country estates in England and Ireland. The Irish estates had been neglected by the 3rd and 4th Marquises. Wallace, accompanied by his wife and son, visited Lisburn, where they entertained the locals in some style. He spent money on a number of public buildings including a school. The family had no house in Lisburn so he built one, Castle House. He also presented the town with a public park. Not unnaturally, he became extremely popular there and sat as Member of Parliament for Lisburn from 1872 until the constituency was amalgamated with another in 1885.[8]

As for Wallace's reception at his estate in Suffolk, Lou Anderson (who had a tailor's business in Broad Street, Orford, from about 1900 and compiled a scrapbook or album which he entitled *Bygone Orford* in which he carefully wrote down the reminiscences of his older customers amongst photos, press cuttings, mourning cards, posters and tickets) recorded this:

> The night when Sir Richard Wallace came to Sudbourne to take over the Estate he was met at the Lodge gates by a large number of his tenants who after

6   Donald Mallett, *The Greatest Collector*, Macmillan, 1979, p. 134.
7   *The Hertford Mawson Letters* (ed. John Ingamells), Wallace Collection, 1981, pp. 90–104.
8   J. F. Burns, 'The Life and Work of Sir Richard Wallace Bart. MP', *Lisburn Historical Society Journal*, vol. 3, 1980, and Hugh Dixon, 'Aspects of the legacy of Sir Richard Wallace in the fabric of Lisburn', *Lisburn Historical Society Journal*, vol. 4, 1982.

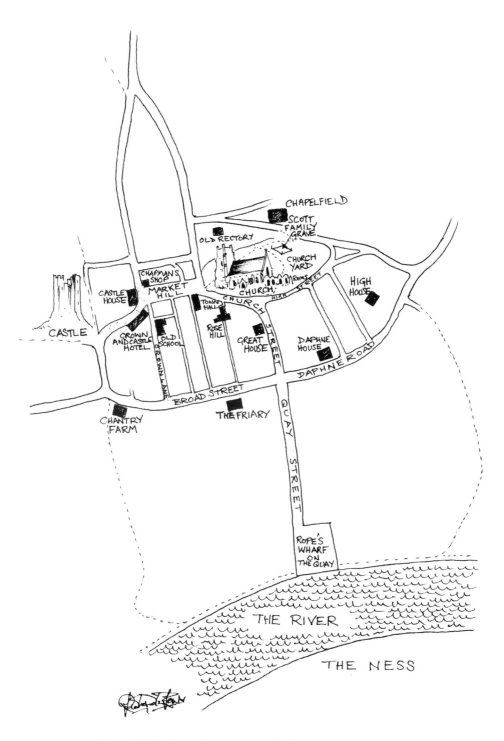

Map of Orford showing houses and places mentioned in text

Plaque with Wallace crest at Chillesford Lodge

presenting an address of Welcome took the horses from the carriage & dragged him to the Hall preceded by a torchlight procession.[9]

The Sudbourne estate had not been neglected, but many houses in the villages of Orford and Sudbourne were improved or rebuilt by Sir Richard Wallace in an ornate but pleasing style. The architect he used was the versatile Frederick Barnes of Ipswich.[10] Dated plaques on the walls allow his work to be identified. The wonder-

9 Lou Anderson's album (in the possession of his grandson, the late John Anderson), p. 112. The impact of this description of Sir Richard Wallace's warm welcome is somewhat diluted by a further account on the same page of a very similar reception being afforded to the brother of Mr A. H. E. Wood, the owner of the estate from 1898. Captain J. Wood had fought in the South African War and had been 'shut up in Ladysmith all the siege'. He, too, 'was met at the Lodge gates by a large number of tenants and drawn to the Hall'.

10 Frederick Barnes (1818–1898) began his practice in Ipswich in 1843. Early in his career he designed the railway stations at Thurston, Stowmarket and Needham Market. In the 1870s he did a great deal of work for Sir Richard Wallace. In addition to his work in the villages of the Sudbourne estate and at the rectory in Orford, he made alterations to Sudbourne Hall in 1872–73 and designed the model farm buildings for the estate's home farm (now Chillesford Lodge). See Edward Martin, 'Chillesford Lodge: a nineteenth century model farm', *Orford & District Local History Bulletin*, Issue 5, 2005, p. 1. The architect who undertook the alterations at Hertford House for Sir Richard Wallace was the 'little-known' Thomas B. Ambler, who, according to Donald Mallett in *The Greatest Collector*, p. 137, also did work for him in Ireland and at Sudbourne, but any buildings for which Ambler may have been responsible in Suffolk have not been identified.

fully fancy house called Three Chimneys at the top of Crown Lane bears the date 1879, but that is probably the date of its adaptation as a reading room housing Miss Crisp's subscription library. There was a British School[11] on the site from 1855 to 1875, but it lost out to the National School[12] opened in 1872 (and still in use today as the Orford Church of England Voluntary Aided Primary School). The National School was built with Sir Richard Wallace's financial assistance at the edge of the village by the track leading to Sudbourne Hall, on a site given for that purpose by the 4th Marquis of Hertford just before he died. After the British School in Crown Lane closed, Sir Richard Wallace bought the building for the benefit of the village (and possibly to placate Miss Crisp who had been active in the management of the British School). He also gave the field next to the school for a village Recreation Ground in 1883, a valuable amenity at a time when the population was growing fast.

Another example of Wallace's active management of the Sudbourne estate was a 'land swap' that he arranged with the church to tidy up the glebe in 1875.[13] The eight acres of glebe land that went with Orford church consisted of a number of very small fields lying between the road to Sudbourne village and the road to Chillesford beyond the White Gates crossroads. Their names are evocative: Sandy Ground, Whyn Field, Clay Pit, First Clay Hill and Arable Piece. There was also a strip of land in Millfield, a relic of the strips in the open fields that had once surrounded the village. After enclosure, the pieces of glebe land were marooned amongst the fields owned by the Sudbourne estate. The glebe exchange swapped the odd fields for an equal area of land in the village owned by the estate but close to the rectory. This was 'part of Little King Field' (the field across which the public footpath runs from Rectory Road to Ferry Road), Kitchen Piece (the site of the Orford Surgery and Chapelfield today) and an extra area of garden for the rectory (now The Old Rectory) including the access track to it, the footpath from Rectory Road to the churchyard.

Sir Richard Wallace took care to maintain Sudbourne's reputation as one of the great sporting estates, renowned for its shooting. The Prince of Wales, later King Edward VII, was a frequent guest, a pleasing echo of the visits to Sudbourne made by the Prince Regent in the 2nd Marquis's time. The friendship between Sir Richard and the Prince of Wales began when the Prince opened the exhibition of Wallace's art

---

11 British schools were established under the auspices of the British and Foreign School Society (set up in 1808) for the education of the poor and labouring classes. They were supported principally by Nonconformists.

12 National schools were the Church of England's educational establishments. The National Society for the Education of the poor in the principles of the Established Church had existed since 1811, but the Education Act of 1870, which set up School Boards to ensure the provision of schools for the poor, seems to have provided the impetus for the church in Orford to open a school.

13 Award of glebe exchange between the Revd John Maynard, and Sir Richard Wallace of Sudbourne Hall, 10 June 1875, SRO (I) FC168/CI1/1.

treasures at the Bethnal Green Museum in 1872. In the summer of 1879 the Prince went to Paris to see the Hertford-British Hospital, built by Wallace as a further tribute to his father. A few months later, in November, the Prince came to shoot at Sudbourne. The visit was of considerable significance in securing Sir Richard Wallace's place in English society. The tenants and workers of the Sudbourne estate were diverted from their normal duties to construct decorated arches across the road at the approach to both villages, Orford and Sudbourne, welcoming the royal visitor.

Three large paintings by the French artist Alfred-Charles-Ferdinand Decaen (1820–1903) now hanging in Orford Town Hall depict this important aspect of life on the estate and show the keepers, drivers, coachmen and even the butler, as well as the guests who made up the shooting parties.

On Sudbourne Hill, 1874, oil painting by Alfred-Charles-Ferdinand Decaen

The first painting, *On Sudbourne Hill, 1874*, shows Sir Richard Wallace accompanied by a large party of aristocratic French guests being greeted by a man, identified as the head gamekeeper, James Harmer, but whose fine livery of green jacket and pale trousers does not appear to be very practical dress for a day's shooting. The foreground is thick with dead pheasants, the gun dogs stand or sit patiently.

The next picture, the finest and most detailed, entitled *A Shooting Luncheon at the Great Wood, Sudbourne, 1876*, is based on a photograph. Lady Wallace steps down from her carriage assisted by her son Edmond. A large table with an immaculate white cloth is set up beneath a majestic oak tree and at a smaller table at the right the food is being prepared (with a plate being placed on the ground for one of the dogs). In the photograph there are just fourteen people. The painting shows twenty-two figures in the foreground and many more, in two groups, in the distance.

Shooting Luncheon at the Great Wood, Sudbourne, 1876,
oil painting by Alfred-Charles-Ferdinand Decaen

Battue de perdreaux dans la comté de Suffolk, 1880,
oil painting by Alfred-Charles-Ferdinand Decaen

The third, painted in 1879 and exhibited at the Paris Salon in 1880 as *Battue de perdreaux dans la comté de Suffolk*, shows the guns in action at Queen Esther's Grove on the way from Orford to Sudbourne church looking over towards the windmill (demolished in 1913) and the castle. Rather surprisingly, it records a shooting accident. The group in the right foreground consists of James Harmer, the head keeper, and another man, in a light-coloured coat, tending John Good (a gamekeeper and warrener on the estate) 'who had an eye shot'.

John Murray Scott is said to be depicted in each of the pictures.[14]

14 Information from an undated (*c.* 1930s) note in the Orford Museum archive, the Wallace Collection Archive, the article in *Apollo Magazine* by Sir Francis Watson (Director of the Wallace Collection) cited in n. 5 above, and *White's Directory, 1874*, entry on Sudbourne. See also an article by R. A. Roberts, 'In the Spacious Days at Orford', *East Anglian Daily Times*, 28 December 1932, and Donald Mallett, *The Greatest Collector*, Macmillan, 1979, p. 158. Donald Mallett is of the opinion that all three pictures were painted from photographs.

5

The Maynard and Scott Families and Life in Orford

When the rector of Sudbourne with Orford, the Revd John Maynard, died in 1877 having held the living for thirty-five years, it seems likely that John Murray Scott recommended his clergyman brother, Edward Scott, then only twenty-seven years old, to Sir Richard Wallace to be Maynard's successor.

Although since the time of Queen Elizabeth I the Crown had been the patron of the living of Sudbourne with Orford (it had originally been the 'prior and convent' of Ely),[1] previous rectors had also been chaplains to the Marquises of Hertford, and it is probable that the views of Sir Richard Wallace would have been taken into account when the post came to be filled. *Crockford's Clerical Directory* of 1877 tells us that Edward Scott attended Gloucester Theological College and was ordained priest in 1874, when he became a curate at the fine church of St Mary Redcliffe, Bristol.

Between John Murray Scott and Edward Scott, was Dr Scott's second son, Douglas Alexander Scott. He was a soldier who served in the Afghan War, the Egyptian War and the Sudan with the Royal Engineers, ending his career as a General in charge of the Coast Defences of the Eastern Command.[2]

Dr John Scott's fourth son, Donald Malcolm Scott (who used just the name Malcolm), was a stockbroker. In 1898 he married an Orford girl, Ann Elizabeth (Bessie) Maynard, the daughter of Walter Fawkes Maynard, the clergyman son of the Revd John Maynard.[3]

As we have seen, Walter Fawkes Maynard had been his father's curate at Sudbourne with Orford for ten years and may have been expected to follow him as rector, but he died of tuberculosis, aged only forty-three, in 1874, predeceasing his father and leaving a widow, Louisa, and four children. Louisa was from a Suffolk family, the Bloomfields (or Blomfields) who lived at Great Glemham, a few miles to the north east of Orford. After they had to leave the rectory, the Maynards lived in Great House in Church Street, Orford. In the early nineteenth century the house had been a hotel but it had been purchased from the Sudbourne estate by the Maynard

---

1 R. A. Roberts, *'Oreford-Nigh-the-Seas'*, Richard Clay, Bungay, 1935, p. 59.
2 Obituary in the *Daily Telegraph*, February 1924 (copy in Wallace Collection Archive, file 38). Apparently he retired rather earlier than he had intended, in 1909, having failed to gain promotion to the rank of Lt-General (information supplied by Martin Cardew).
3 See pp. 18, 19, above.

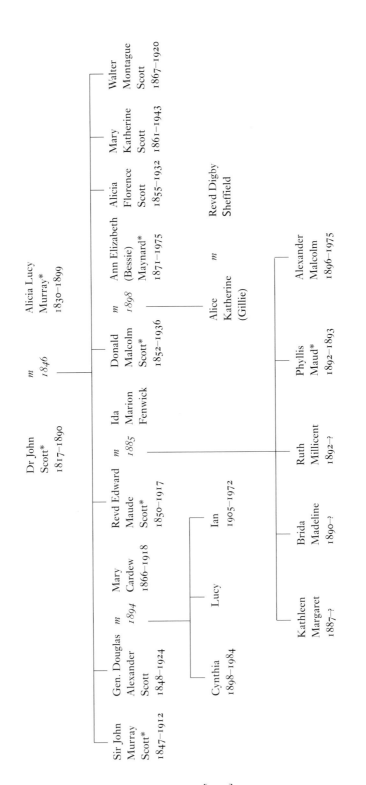

Scott family tree

Those marked * are buried in Orford churchyard

family and named after their plantation house in the West Indies. When the children were young, the Maynards were short of money, but later, in the twentieth century, Mrs Louisa Maynard and her three surviving children, Bessie Scott, Dr John Maynard and Miss Mary Maynard, were generous donors of items to the church, not least the east window and the two paintings which hang as altarpieces in the St Nicholas Chapel and above the main altar.

The next two children of John and Alicia Scott were girls, Alicia Florence and Mary Katherine. Another son was born in 1867, twenty years after John Murray Scott. This brother, Walter Montague Scott, and his two sisters remained, like their eldest brother, unmarried.[4]

At that time, the Scotts seem to have been a close and united family.

So, probably thanks to his brother's influence, the Revd Edward Scott came to live in Orford rectory. *Crockford's Clerical Directory* gives some details of the living in 1877: the population of Orford was 1022 and the tithe £317. Sudbourne's population was 532 but the tithe produced £502. The gross income was given as £846 (about £36,600 at today's values) but this could be a little misleading; by 1901 *Crockford* starts giving a net figure for the tithes (albeit one provided by the clergy themselves), and at that date Sudbourne with Orford's net figure was £293, which would be about £17,000 today. *Kelly's Directory* for Suffolk of 1892 gives the probably more realistic net figure of £369, some £21,320 today – a comfortable, but by no means enormous amount. The rectory had been rebuilt in 1832 (see p. 125 below) and was enlarged in 1878 to plans by the architect Frederick Barnes.[5] It became a comfortable and elegant family home. Evidence of the 'Wallace connection' is to be found in the fact that the door furniture on the entrance to the rectory is identical to some in Hertford House.

Bessie Scott (Malcolm's wife) lived to the great age of a hundred and three, and in her reminiscences, written down by one of her great-granddaughters in the early 1970s,[6] she says that the appointment of the bachelor Edward Scott to the good living of Sudbourne with Orford excited some comment in the press at the time. Yet the new rector became firm friends with her family, the Maynards, and often sent his coachmen to ask if the ladies would like to drive to the nearby towns of Woodbridge or Saxmundham, offers which they accepted gratefully.

Edward Scott was soon fully involved in the life of Orford. He enjoyed sailing and was a member of the Regatta committee. When out on the river one Saturday

4   Walter did become engaged in 1920, but he died of cancer before the marriage could take place (information supplied by Martin Cardew).
5   Mortgages for the enlargement of the Rectory, 15 May 1878 (£325) and 2 September 1878 (£218), SRO(I) FC168/C9/2 and FC168/C9/3.
6   Mr Nigel Sheffield, Malcolm and Bessie Scott's grandson, has provided the Orford Museum archive with a copy of the memoir.

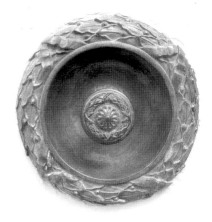

Brass door knob and bell pull at Orford rectory (now The Old Rectory)

afternoon in July 1880 with Thomas Lloyd Place (Orford's surgeon) and the Revd J. S. Upcher (a former curate at Orford) he had the misfortune to find and retrieve the body of Mr Neighbour, the schoolmaster and organist, who had accidentally drowned when bathing.[7] As chairman of the committee of Orford School, Edward Scott stepped into the breach. He made the following entry in the school log book, dated 4 October 1880, the day on which the replacement schoolmaster took up his duties:

> Mr Henry Neighbour, school master, was drowned on the 17th of July 1880. Owing to this unfortunate circumstance the log book has not been entered up. The school was closed on the 13th August and reopened on the 13th September. The chairman of the committee visited the school daily in the absence of a master and at times took classes for instruction.[8]

Members of the Scott family were very much in evidence in Orford. John Murray Scott was at Sudbourne Hall when Sir Richard Wallace was in residence. Other brothers and sisters of Edward Scott came frequently from their home in London to visit. At the time of the 1881 census the rector's sister, Mary Scott, and their maternal grandfather, George St Vincent Murray, were staying, if not living, at the rectory.

In 1885 Edward Scott married a wealthy woman, Ida Marion Fenwick. The Orford church banns book tells us that she was 'of the parish of St Paul's, Knightsbridge in

7 *Woodbridge Reporter*, 22 July 1880. The report says that 'when his body was brought ashore . . . about 200 followed from the riverside to the school-house' (John Anderson, 'Danger – River Ore!', *Orford & District Local History Bulletin*, Issue 7, 2006, p. 2).

8 Orford National Mixed School log book, 1872–1902, SRO(I) FC168/M1/3.

London'. Her father later lived in Bournemouth. The rector and his wife soon began to produce a family. Kathleen was born in 1887, Brida in 1890 and twin girls, Ruth and Phyllis in 1892.

The soldier brother, Douglas, does not seem to have participated in Orford affairs in any way, but he was married to Mary Cardew, who, prior to her marriage, was a professional musician. Edward Scott's successor as rector was the Revd Frederick Anstruther Cardew, a member of her family.[9]

Malcolm Scott was nineteen years older than Bessie Maynard. She had this to say about him before their marriage, and her anecdote incidentally reveals that the Scotts were a prosperous family:

[Bessie] and her sister looked on Malcolm Scott as a kind of uncle who gave them presents and devised wonderful outings for them all including the boys [her two brothers]. They, the boys, were met *en route* back to school after the holidays and given a treat in London which they greatly enjoyed but young Jack Maynard would privately think it was a lot of money to spend and they would rather have had the money. The Maynards of course had little money.

Revd Edward Scott on horseback at Orford rectory, early 1880s,
with his beard grown by royal command

9 Information supplied by the late Dr Peter Cardew, the Revd F. A. Cardew's son.

When Bessie married her 'kind of uncle', thus uniting the families of the present and past rectors, on 24 August 1898 in Orford church, the account of the wedding in the *Ipswich Journal* (dated Saturday 27 August) tells us that:

the sacred edifice was beautifully decorated and there was a crowded congregation. Miss A. F. Scott, sister of the bridegroom, gave a musical selection during the assembling of the congregation, and played the 'Wedding March' at the close of the service. The service was fully choral, and well rendered by the surpliced choir. The hymns were 'Lead us, Heavenly Father', 'The Voice that breathed o'er Eden', 'O perfect love' and a very beautiful hymn specially written for the occasion by H. Franklin which was set to an effective tune by Miss Scott . . . The choir were entertained by Mr D. M. Scott with an excellent dinner at the Crown and Castle Hotel. The village was profusely decorated.

Two of the rector's three little daughters, Kathleen and Brida, were the child bridesmaids. Mrs Maynard's brother-in-law, the Revd Charles Raymond (who was also Bessie's godfather and had been a contributor to the church restoration appeal), officiated. The best man was John Murray Scott (see the frontispiece and p. 79 below).

Although the Scotts' parents, Dr John Scott and Alicia Scott, lived in Chandos Street just off Cavendish Square in London after they left Boulogne, they were buried in Orford churchyard when they died in 1890 and 1899 respectively. The large and elaborately carved cross marking their grave (and that of John Murray Scott) is in the middle of the square plot marked off with a low iron rail halfway along the path from the rectory gate to the Norman ruins at the east end of the church. Malcolm was buried there in 1936 aged eighty-four. His wife, Bessie, was the last Scott to be buried in the plot in 1975.

A letter in the Wallace Collection archive written in 1965 by Alexander Scott, Edward Scott's son, gives a picture of his father and uncle and the extent to which the Scott family were integrated into life at Sudbourne Hall.

My father was a very good shot and was nearly always included among the guns at Sudbourne Hall though I see no sign of him in the picture of the shooting lunch [here he is referring to one of the large pictures which hang in Orford Town Hall, see pp. 36, 37 above] . . . my uncle John Murray Scott . . . was a commanding figure of some 6' 4" in height and sported mutton chop whiskers as also did my father until at a shoot at Sudbourne the then Prince of Wales later King Edward VII told my father that he thought all parsons should wear beards – my father taking this as a Royal Command promptly grew one and became surprisingly like King Edward.

He also mentions the family's musical talents:

> Mary . . . was the singer of the family and sang duets with John McCormack
> [the enormously popular tenor, who was a protégé of John Murray Scott] and
> my Aunt Alicia would have accompanied them. John Murray played the cello
> and Walter the violin – my father also had a very good singing voice – Malcolm
> and Douglas as far as I know were quite unmusical.[10]

In fact he did his uncle Douglas an injustice. The general used to sing at concerts both
in India and at home in England. The violin played by Walter was a Stradivarius.[11]
Bessie Scott recalled the hospitality at Sudbourne Hall when she was a small child:

> The young Maynards used to visit Sudbourne and receive little gifts from Lady
> Wallace and had to thank her prettily in French as she spoke very little English
> . . . Once the family had been invited to lunch and it was all very grand and a lit-
> tle overpowering for two little girls who usually had the plainest of food. Bessie was
> given a beautiful-looking meringue. She was so overawed by its magnificence that
> she waited for a moment before eating it. To her speechless horror it was
> whisked away. Poor little girl. At Christmas time the village children were enter-
> tained at the Hall with a huge party and Christmas tree and the little Maynards
> were just lookers on and wistfully watched the village children receive their
> gifts. However their turn came and Lady Wallace was very generous to them too.

She also had this to say about a figure who does not usually receive more than a line
or two in publications about Sir Richard Wallace; his son, Edmond Richard Wallace:

> Sir Richard and Lady Wallace had one son who was born in Paris in 1840, and
> therefore a French subject. He joined the French army in 1860 and was with his
> company at the Siege of Paris and served with distinction and was made a
> Chevalier of the Legion of Honour. He went with his parents to England and
> became a naturalised Englishman in 1872, but his heart was in Paris in more
> ways than one, having fallen in love with a lady he could not marry but with
> whom he lived and had four children. He quarrelled with his father and this
> greatly distressed his mother. Bessie's mother [Mrs Louisa Maynard] told her
> that Capt Wallace was an exceedingly charming young man. He died in 1887
> being only forty-seven years old.

10 Wallace Collection Archive, file 38 (Family of John Murray Scott).
11 Information supplied by Martin Cardew.

As we have seen, Edmond Wallace is depicted in the painting of a shooting luncheon at Sudbourne, helping his mother descend from a carriage. He was a great disappointment to his parents. It would appear that when Sir Richard Wallace moved to England, he hoped that his son would marry into an English family and settle in Lisburn at Castle House. With the help of the Prime Minister, Benjamin Disraeli, Sir Richard also hoped that Edmond would, exceptionally, be enabled to inherit his father's title in spite of his illegitimate birth. In 1875 Disraeli wrote a memorandum to Queen Victoria suggesting it, but the Queen would not countenance the proposal. In any event, at the very time when his father was taking active steps to try to establish an English Wallace dynasty, Edmond Wallace's interests, as Bessie Scott recalled, were firmly centred on Paris. He had fallen in love with an actress, Amélie-Suzanne Gall, and in 1872 the first of their children, George, was born. Thereafter, at two-yearly intervals, his family grew. The next boy, Henry, was followed by Edmond, born in 1876. The fourth child, a daughter named Georgette, completed the family in 1878.[12] By 1879 Sir Richard Wallace and his only son were virtually estranged. When, in November that year, the Prince of Wales came to Sudbourne to join a shooting party, Edmond Wallace was not there. Instead, the 'younger generation' was represented by John Murray Scott and his two sisters.[13]

In 1884, Sir Richard Wallace, who was not in good health, sold the Sudbourne estate to a banker, Mr Arthur Heywood, and moved to live in London.

It would seem that the decision to leave Sudbourne was a sudden one. The principal tenants of the estate commissioned the Suffolk-born artist, W. R. Symonds, to paint a portrait of Sir Richard. The sittings took place in London during 1885 and the presentation was made to Sir Richard and Lady Wallace at Hertford House in 1886, two years after they had actually moved away. There are prints of the photograph taken on that occasion in the archives of Orford Museum (the New Orford Town Trust collection) and the Wallace Collection. The portrait of Sir Richard Wallace, which is on display at the Wallace Collection, was exhibited at the Royal Academy that year.

The sale of the Sudbourne estate seems to have escaped the notice of most of those who have written about the Hertfords, Sir Richard Wallace and the Wallace Collection.[14] It was indeed a fairly minor matter in the story of the art collection, but

12 J. F. Burns, 'The Life and Work of Sir Richard Wallace Bart. MP', *Lisburn Historical Society Journal*, vol. 3, 1980. See also Peter Hughes, *The Founders of the Wallace Collection*, Wallace Collection, 1981, pp. 52 and 54, and Bernard Falk, *'Old Q's' Daughter*, Hutchinson, 1937 (reprinted Cedric Chivers Ltd, 1970) p. 295.

13 Donald Mallett, *The Greatest Collector*, Macmillan, 1979, p. 170.

14 Because the sale in 1884 is overlooked, a number of books contain the statement that Lady Wallace in 1890, and then John Murray Scott in 1913, inherited the Sudbourne estate, which was not the

The Sudbourne estate tenants presenting a portrait to Sir Richard Wallace at Hertford House, 9 August 1886. *From the left* Sir Richard Wallace, Lady Wallace, John Murray Scott, Revd Edward Scott, William Chambers (Ferry Farm, Sudbourne), William Wilson (Raydon Hall), Francis Keer (Brick Kiln Farm, Iken), William Toller (Richmond Farm, Gedgrave), Henry Brinkley (Crag Farm, Sudbourne), William Estaugh (Church Farm, Sudbourne), Edward Rope (with white beard, Rope's Quay, Orford), Francis Wase (Church Farm, Chillesford), W. R. Symonds (the artist).

for the people of Orford, in particular, it must have been seen as a momentous change, coming at what was already an unsettling time. A piece of reforming legislation, the Municipal Corporations Act of 1883, meant that Orford was to lose the status it had held since 1579 as a borough with a mayor and corporation. This actually happened

case. See, e.g., Donald Mallett, *The Greatest Collector*, Macmillan, 1979, Foreword, pp. xiii and 150 (where he asserts that Sir John Murray Scott sold the estate to Kenneth Mackenzie Clark, Lord Clark's father; in fact Clark purchased it from Mr A. H. E. Wood (Arthur Heywood's successor) in 1904) and p. 183; Peter Hughes, *The Founders of the Wallace Collection*, Wallace Collection, 1981, p. 58; Bernard Falk, *'Old Q's' Daughter*, Hutchinson, 1937 (Cedric Chivers Ltd reprint, 1970) p. 288, also cited in Matthew Harrison, *An Anglican Adventure, The History of St George's Anglican Church, Paris*, 2005, p. 55. The Sudbourne estate had five different owners in the fifty years following Sir Richard Wallace's departure. Many of the farms and village properties have been sold, but stability has returned to the core of the estate, albeit much reduced in size, which is now split between Chillesford Lodge/Newton and Sudbourne Park/Gedgrave. Each portion remains in the hands of the families who acquired them in the 1920s and 1930s, the Watsons and the Greenwells.

Photograph of the widowed Lady Wallace

in 1886, so William Toller, Orford's last mayor, standing in the foreground of the photograph, knew, when he went up to London with the party from Suffolk, that he was soon to be history.

We have seen that Sir Richard Wallace had been a very generous landlord, so the severance of the 130-year connection between the Sudbourne estate and the Hertford family must have caused some anxiety locally. It was the end of an era. One element of continuity was to be found in the person of the rector, Edward Scott. Secure in the freehold of his living, the departure of his brother from Sudbourne Hall did not affect his occupancy of the rectory.

Sir Richard Wallace's later years were dogged by illness, including depression. These troubles were exacerbated by the premature death of his son Edmond from heart disease in 1887, thereby ending any remaining hope of a reconciliation. Sir Richard returned to Paris to live a reclusive life at Bagatelle which he had repaired and remodelled after the damage it had suffered during the siege of Paris. His French wife, Lady Wallace, remained in England, helped in her everyday life, no doubt, by John Murray Scott.

It seems that Sir Richard Wallace intended to leave his collection to the British nation and took some steps to work out the details of his intended gift.[15] However, he died in Paris in July 1890, two days before Dr John Scott also died.

Perhaps this coincidence helped to cement the relationship between Lady Wallace and the Scott family. Later that year Mrs Scott and her daughters took a holiday in Brighton with Lady Wallace, the first of many shared holidays. The widowed Lady Wallace continued to live in London at Hertford House and became even more dependent on John Murray Scott (who also lived at Hertford House). Mrs Scott or her daughters would visit Lady Wallace every day from their home in nearby Chandos Street.[16] The Scotts clearly considered themselves to be her most intimate friends. The unflattering photograph of the seventy-five-year-old Lady Wallace now in the National Portrait Gallery was taken in 1894 by Walter Scott.

15 Peter Hughes, *The Founders of the Wallace Collection*, Wallace Collection, 1981, p. 54.
16 Transcript of the London *Evening Standard* report of the first day's proceedings in the case of *Capron v Scott*, 24 June 1913, p. 3 (Wallace Collection Archive, file 38).

6

Restoration at Sudbourne Church and an Emergency at Orford

When Sir Richard Wallace took up residence in Sudbourne Hall, Sudbourne church was in a very dilapidated state. A thorough restoration was undertaken in 1878–79, largely at his expense. The cost was said to have been £2,000[1] (or £100,000 at today's prices), which seems to be something of a bargain. A temporary iron church was erected so that services could be held whilst the work was going on. The architect was Frederick Barnes who had been used by Wallace for other work around the Sudbourne estate and by Edward Scott for the enlargement of Orford rectory. The east end of the church was entirely rebuilt because it was beyond repair, but the rest of the church was treated sensitively. The windows, for example, which display almost every period of church architecture, were restored carefully. A rather nice touch is the little spire, a 'Hertfordshire spike', perhaps added to the tower as a tribute to Sir Richard Wallace's forebears[2] (see the pictures on p. 78 below). A small brass plate on the organ case records the fact that the instrument (which is said to have come from Sudbourne Hall) was the gift of Sir Richard Wallace. The lectern Bible was presented by Lady Wallace.

After that job was finished, it was Orford's turn. In 1881 drawings were produced at the request of Sir Richard Wallace by the eminent architect George Edmund Street[3] for a complete scheme of restoration for Orford church. Street, best known as

1 Manuscript copy by R. A. Roberts of a letter from E. A. Rope dated *c.*1880 which also gives details of 'The Remarkable Find of Coins at Sudbourne Church' (Orford Museum Archive). A hoard of 2,500 silver coins dating from the reigns of Henry II, King John, Henry III and William the Lion of Scotland was discovered under the floor of the north aisle while the work was being done. Although the find was reported to and examined by Dr Taylor, the Curator of the Ipswich Museum, all the coins have now disappeared: R. A. Roberts, *'Oreford-Nigh-the-Seas'*, Richard Clay, Bungay, 1935, p. 14.

2 Roy Tricker, *All Saints Church Sudbourne Suffolk, a brief history and guide*, 1987, pp. 2–3. The 'spike' could be said to be a return to the status quo. Although eighteenth-century maps of Suffolk (Kirby, 1736, and Hodskinson, 1783) and the picture of Sudbourne church in the mid-nineteenth century, p. 78, show just a tower (albeit, in the case of the watercolour, with a small tiled conical roof), the map of Orford Ness from the time of Queen Elizabeth I in the British Library (see p. 23 above) clearly shows Sudbourne church with a tower and a large spire.

3 His drawings were kept in the church until 1967 when Major Steuart Gratton, the churchwarden, wrote a letter to the church architect of the time, A. D. R. Caroe, telling him that the Diocesan Care of Churches Committee had noticed the drawings on a visit and suggested that they should go

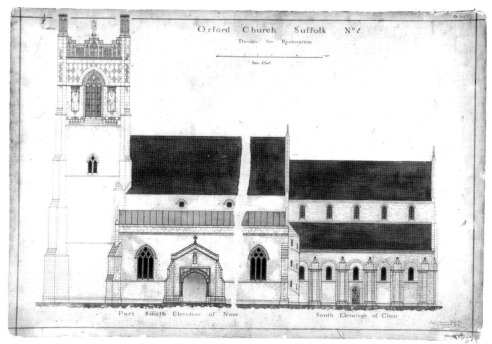

Part South Elevation of Nave   South Elevation of Choir

Drawing for restoration of Orford church by G. E. Street

the architect of the Royal Courts of Justice in the Strand, devised a breathtakingly ambitious proposal which involved re-incorporating the ruined Norman chancel into the church and rebuilding a huge and lofty tower. Street's plan was not acted on by Sir Richard Wallace.

His only further contribution to the parish churches before he left in 1884 was a thorough redecoration and cleaning programme back at Sudbourne church which caused the church to be closed again for a month in 1882. A dado of shiny Minton tiles and an elaborate stencilled decorative pattern were applied to the sanctuary walls. When the church was reopened on 24 September the preacher was the rector, Edward Scott.[4]

There is no record of any real concern about the state of the fabric of Orford church during the first fifteen years of Edward Scott's incumbency. There was some embellishment, but not, it seems, repair.

In April 1888 there was a fund-raising event ('a most successful concert given in the

to the Library of the Royal Institute of British Architects. They were deposited at the RIBA, from which small photocopies have been obtained for Orford Museum. The RIBA Library Drawings Collection is now at the Victoria and Albert Museum.

4 *All Saints Church Sudbourne Suffolk, a brief history and guide*, p. 5. For Sir Richard Wallace's involvement with the building of a new Anglican church in Paris, see n. 6 to chapter 8 below.

Schoolroom by Miss Place, assisted by numerous friends') to pay for 'a handsome six-light central brass corona . . . to complete the lighting, which will now be thoroughly effective'. The corona was duly hung in the centre of the nave and lit for the first time on Sunday evening, 2 September.[5]

A gable cross to replace the one removed by William Dowsing in 1644 (see pp. 14, 15 above) was 'placed on the east gable of the nave' by the Bishop of Norwich on 10 March 1890.[6]

At Easter 1891 the rector, his mother and sisters gave the large brass eagle lectern, which stands in front of the screen in the nave, and the cross and candlesticks, still in use on the St Nicholas chapel altar, in memory of Dr John Scott.

There is no surviving terrier for a period of fifteen years after that of 1879 (see p. 20 above), but in the 1894 terrier many new church furnishings were itemized. The only hint of possible trouble was that the organ was no longer described as 'elegant' but 'now fallen into decay'. The silver from the Marquis of Hertford and Mrs Fawkes's gift of a frontal and linen were listed, then the following, showing that the services at Orford were becoming more elaborate and the church interior was being embellished, following the general trend towards more ritual in the Church of England:

An oak altar. Two oak Glastonbury chairs.[7] Oak credence table.[8] One red velvet altar cloth and super frontal[9] with worked cross and orphreys.[10] One violet altar cloth with worked I H S and white silk orphreys. Three red kneeling mats.

5 *Sudbourn and Orford Parish Magazine*, June and September 1888. The corona cannot be the very handsome brass chandelier which now hangs in the chancel, which has four arms each with four candle holders. This is listed in the 1902 terrier as the gift of Mrs Scott, which could mean either the rector's mother or his wife.

6 A handsome leather-bound presentation copy of *The Priest to the Altar, or aids to the devout celebration of Holy Communion chiefly after the ancient English use of Sarum*, 3rd edn, 1879, is inscribed in Edward Scott's handwriting:

To the Right Reverend John Lord Bishop of the Diocese in grateful remembrance of the 10th March 1890 when he placed the Cross on the East gable of the Nave of the church of St Bartholomew, Orford, Suffolk. Edward M Scott Rector of Sudbourn & Orford.

The book was found in a second-hand bookseller's in the 1970s by Nick Groves of Norwich who brought it to the attention of Margaret Poulter, the honorary curator of Orford Museum.

7 A type of chair assembled by means of wooden pins, with X-shaped legs joined by a cross bar, which usually stands in the chancel.

8 A side table in the sanctuary on which the bread, wine and water for the Communion service are placed.

9 A band of material, usually fringed, overlapping the top of the frontal on the altar.

10 Embroidered bands usually decorating vestments such as copes or chasubles (the outer vestment worn by a priest when celebrating the Communion), but here decorating altar frontals.

Three violet kneeling mats. Red white and violet silk chalice veil,[11] burse,[12] pulpit fall[13] and four alms bags. Green chalice veil, burse and four alms bags. Set of white linen for use in the Communion Service.

Brass cross and two candle sticks, brass eagle lectern, brass font ewer, set of brass bound books, all inscribed as given to the church in memory of the late John Scott MD the father of the present rector.

Two pairs of brass vases. Brass altar desk. Two lamp standards each bearing four lamps. Bracket bearing one lamp. One corona bearing six lamps. Five other coronas each bearing four lamps. And two other coronas each bearing three lamps. One iron chest containing registers. One oak vestment cupboard.

Many of the new ornaments and furnishings were manufactured and sold by the firm of Jones & Willis of Birmingham and, because they are still in use, may be identified from the catalogue, which confidently stated:

For orders amounting to £40 or upwards, Jones & Willis respectfully inform their numerous patrons that to save time and trouble they will be happy to send a competent person to take Orders and Measurements, with Samples of Materials, Free of Expense, to any part of the Kingdom . . . To secure excellence and durability, the greatest attention will be given to the manufacture of the Articles, and thus they hope to obtain the approbation of those who may favour them with their orders.[14]

The Glastonbury chairs cost 47s 6d each. The credence table was £5 5s. The brass cross ('jewelled and engraved (without figure)', 2ft 9ins, 10 guineas) and two candlesticks (18ins, £3 5s each) are the ones still in use in the St Nicholas Chapel (and are identical to those in Sudbourne church). The large brass eagle lectern was one of the most expensive items made by the firm, at £100. The lectern platform, though not listed in the terrier, must have been acquired at the same time, and was priced at £8 10s. The brass font ewer, a fine object in an interesting, angular Arts and Crafts style, cost £2 10s. The lamp coronas (adapted to electricity and still in use in the church) were £5 17s 6d for the three lamp model, £7 15s for four lamps and £10 10s

11 A square of coloured material used to cover the chalice and paten when they are not in use during the Communion service.
12 An 'envelope' made of stiffened material in which the corporal (a linen square placed on the altar on which to stand the bread and wine for consecration in the Communion service) is kept.
13 An embroidered, coloured cloth which hangs from the book rest on the pulpit.
14 *An illustrated catalogue of some of the articles in church furniture, manufactured by Jones & Willis,* 57th edn, Birmingham and London, 1875.

Orford's £100 lectern

for six lamps. It should be remembered that £1 in 1894 is worth about £60 today.

None of the articles acquired for liturgical use in Orford church could be described as anything other than 'middle of the road'. It is clear that the rector and congregation steered a careful course between the usages of the High Church Anglo-Catholics and the Low Church Evangelicals.

The churchwardens' accounts show that from 1885 an organist was being paid £20 a year. He was William Belgrove, the headmaster of Orford School.[15] There was no new organ listed in the terrier; perhaps he struggled to play on the 'decayed' instrument (see pp. 52 above and 67 below) until the new organ listed in the 1908 terrier

15 Churchwardens' Book containing disbursements 1866–1920, SRO(I) FC168/E5/2. A previous (apparently unpaid) organist had also been Orford's schoolmaster. The newspaper report of the inquest on the unfortunate Henry Neighbour, who drowned in the river (see p. 42 above), stated that 'Mr Neighbour was organist at the church, and he was greatly missed on Sunday, the services being conducted without the aid of any instrumental music'.

arrived (see p. 94 below). There was certainly a flourishing choir and its members knew how to have a good time. In June and September 1888 the parish magazine records first, the church choir's annual concert ('proceeds devoted to providing a treat for the choir in the shape of a tea which took place on 17 May when an enjoyable evening was passed'), and then the annual choir outing enjoyed by the two choirs of Orford and Sudbourne churches, a boat trip from Orford Quay to Aldeburgh. 'The homeward cruise was enlivened by several glees and songs . . . ringing cheers were given on landing at the Quay before dispersing homewards.'[16]

Then an alarming state of affairs was revealed. According to the appeal brochure put out in 1894, in 1892 it was discovered that 'the tie beams of the roof of the nave were in a very dilapidated and dangerous condition'.[17] Drastic action was required: 'On this account it was deemed absolutely necessary to at once abandon that part of the church.'

A public meeting was held on 6 July 1892 in Orford School and an Orford Church Restoration Committee was elected. Its proceedings are recorded in a leather-bound book. The chairman was the rector, Edward Scott, the treasurer was William Toller. The committee consisted of Arthur Heywood (the new owner of Sudbourne Hall), Edward Rope, William Chapman (grocer and draper, also oyster merchant), Thomas Lloyd Place (the doctor, who lived at High House) and William Wilson. The secretary was Walter H. Rope, Edward Rope's son.[18] Some of these names will be recognized as members of the party which presented the portrait to Sir Richard Wallace six years before (see p. 47 above).

At the first meeting of the Committee on 15 July the chairman was 'authorised to call upon the secretary of the Society for the [Protection] of Ancient Buildings to ascertain whether the late Mr G. E. Street's plans would meet with the approval of his Society and to ask whether his society would advise the appointment of the late Mr Street's son [A. E. Street] for the carrying out of the work'. The minute of the second meeting one month later simply states: 'The rector was authorised to see Mr Micklethwaite (the architect selected by the Society for the [Protection] of Ancient Buildings) and ask him to inspect the church and give a rough estimate.'

Thereby hangs a tale. The SPAB, founded by William Morris in 1877, had begun a vigorous campaign against the over-restoration perpetrated by the likes of Sir George Gilbert Scott and G. E. Street in so many churches. By the late nineteenth century it was realized that, particularly for fine medieval churches such as Orford's,

16 See n. 5 above.
17 Incorporated Church Building Society file 9830, Lambeth Palace Library.
18 Names from Orford Church Restoration Minute Book, occupations and residences from *Kelly's Directory of Suffolk, 1892*. The minute book, incorrectly, refers to the Society for the *Preservation* of Ancient Buildings.

'conservation' was a more appropriate approach than full-blooded restoration. It is interesting, and perhaps fortunate, that the SPAB was the first port of call for the Orford Church Restoration Committee. The reason may have been the furious criticism that proposals by A. E. Street for the restoration of Blythburgh church in the early 1880s had attracted from the SPAB.[19]

John Thomas Micklethwaite (1843–1906) had been a pupil of George Gilbert Scott in 1862, but had won the approval of the SPAB by 1892. Micklethwaite was surveyor to the Dean and Chapter of Westminster Abbey in 1898 and was responsible for a restoration of the west front and south transept of the Abbey. In 1901 he became architect to St George's Chapel, Windsor. He was clearly an architect of the highest calibre. Four of his drawings for Orford (of the nave and north aisle roofs and the porch) are still in the possession of the church. He does not appear to have undertaken any other work in Suffolk.

At the next meeting of the Orford Restoration Committee in September 1892 Mr Micklethwaite's report was read and the treasurer was authorized

> to open a banking account with Messrs Gurney & Co, Woodbridge at the same time asking them to hang a subscription card in the Bank at Woodbridge It was decided to get appeal and subscription cards printed and distributed as soon as possible, also to board up bays between the middle and south aisles.

To quote again from the appeal brochure: 'The south aisle was therefore boarded off and Divine Service is now held there.' The churchwardens' accounts show the expenditure of £7 0s 9d for 'alterations in church'.[20]

The photograph of the south aisle from that time when it was used as the main church is full of interest. An extra chair has been placed beside the end of each pew and rows of chairs crammed in at the back. The big brass eagle lectern given only the year before in memory of the rector's father almost certainly posed something of a problem in the much reduced space available and is to be seen in the centre of the aisle in front of the altar. The Commandments and Lord's Prayer boards which had been behind the main altar are rather awkwardly repositioned at the angles of the east wall. The altar must surely be the one listed in the terrier and it is interesting to speculate whether it was originally intended for the main altar and transferred to the south aisle as a temporary measure, or whether it was placed there before the aisle was boarded off, as an improvement in place of the vestry cupboard shown on Davy's 1832 plan

19 Anne Riches, *Victorian Church Building and Restoration in Suffolk*, a supplement to H. Munro Cautley's *Suffolk Churches*, The Boydell Press, 1982, pp. 381–2.
20 Churchwardens' Book containing disbursements 1866–1920, SRO(I) FC168/E5/2.

The crowded south aisle of Orford church when it was partitioned off to serve
as the main church

The former reredos now incorporated into a pew

(see p. 13 above). The carved panel serving as a retable behind the altar will be recognized, as it now forms the front of the massive free-standing pew which at the moment is situated against the south aisle wall. A photograph in H. Munro Cautley's *Suffolk Churches* (1937)[21] shows it over in the north east of the church, facing into the sanctuary and filling the space which now gives access to the Chapel of Our Lady in the Wall (see p. 131 below). Later it served as the verger's pew and stood in front of the tower arch. The carved saints on either side of Christ in Majesty in the centre panel are Saints Stephen, Philip, Jude, Andrew, John and Matthew.[22]

The photograph also records the final appearance of the eighteenth-century pulpit, moved, minus its canopy, to a temporary position in the south aisle. For the fate of the pews and pulpit, see pp. 85 and 121 below. The red altar frontal in the photograph is still in use, following some adjustments, in Sudbourne church.

21 H. Munro Cautley, *Suffolk Churches and their Treasures*, first published 1937, 4th rev. edn, The Boydell Press, 1975, p. 163.
22 D. P. Mortlock, *The Popular Guide to Suffolk Churches No. 3 East Suffolk*, Acorn Editions, 1992, p. 141.

7

Work Gets Under Way

Preparation of the plans and specification requested in March 1893 took nearly a year. (Sadly, also in March 1893, Phyllis Maud, one of Edward's and Ida's twin daughters died, aged eight and a half months, and was buried in the churchyard near the grave of her grandfather, Dr John Scott.)

When they were ready, the building plans were submitted to the Restoration Committee on February 1894. The estimate for the complete works of restoration was the very large sum of £10,000 (about £600,000 in today's money). A faculty[1] was obtained in May but it was decided not to start the work until the £4,000 needed for the work on the roof had been raised.

The appeal brochure was prepared, describing the church, the Norman chancel and the tower, the problem with the roof and stating that £1,300 had already been subscribed or promised. 'The Rector and Churchwardens appeal therefore with much confidence to the liberality of the wealthy to assist them in saving this noble edifice from absolute ruin and decay.'[2] There was a list of donations to date. The fund-raising activities were very similar to those we undertake nowadays – a bazaar, a musical entertainment, an appeal box in the church, approaches to the local grandees.

Amounts paid

Revd* & Mrs E. M. Scott	100. 0.0
Big Sale of Work	145. 0.0
Offertories & church box	73.14.6
G. J. Fenwick [Mrs Ida Scott's father]	25. 0.0
W. Toller *	25. 0.0
Mrs Scott (London) [the rector's mother]	20. 0.0
T. L. Place*	10. 0.0
Mrs Maynard [Great House]	10. 0.0
Mr Edward Rope*	10. 0.0
Mr Chapman*	10. 0.0

1 Before any alteration or addition can be made to a church, its land or its contents, it is a legal requirement that a faculty (a dispensation or licence) should be obtained from the bishop's Chancellor.

2 Incorporated Church Building Society file 9830, Lambeth Palace Library.

J. J. Hornby	10. 0.0
Misses Crisp [Rose Hill]	5. 5.0
H. Colmore Dunn	5. 5.0
Revd C. A. Raymond [Mrs Maynard's brother-in-law]	5. 0.0
Ven. Archdeacon Hornby	5. 0.0
Mr & Mrs R. G. Ledger	5. 0.0
Misses Toller	5. 0.0
Mrs G. J. Fenwick [Mrs Ida Scott's mother]	5. 0.0
Collecting cards	
Mrs Cumberlege	13.11.6
Mrs Colbeck	7. 7.0
The Jimcrack minstrels	5. 0.0
Amounts under £5	75. 4.0
	590. 7.0
Amounts promised	
Arthur Heywood*	500. 0.0
Mrs Heywood	100. 0.0
Robert Crisp [Daphne House]	100. 0.0
Bishop of Norwich	20. 0.0
Revd Randolph [the curate]	5. 0.0
Mr J. Martin	5. 0.0
G. Wilson	5. 0.0
Revd B. St Pattrick	2. 2.0
B. E. Pemberton	20. 0.0
Mr & Mrs Courtney	5. 0.0
	762. 2.0

* Committee members

An unwelcome response to the appeal appeared in the *Framlingham Weekly News* of 4 May 1895.[3] The heading was 'Orford Church Restoration':

3   There is a manuscript copy of the letter in the Orford church files.

The Orford Jimcrack Minstrel Troupe, 1894

The following has been addressed to the Committee for Restoration by a recipient of their printed appeal for Subscriptions. —

Leek. May 1st 1895

The Rector & Churchwardens of Orford, Suffolk

Gentlemen,

I have received your circular appealing for subscriptions to 'restore' that precious jewel, your lovely Parish Church. I am referring to the glorious portion of the fabric which remains, as yet, intact and almost as its gifted creators left it. Visiting the Church a year ago I was charmed with the boarded off portion (nave, N. aisle, chancel, tower, S. porch, etc) and pray you to leave it as it is, with such repairs solely as are requisite for its maintenance as a supreme work of art. Surely the disastrous depravation of the south aisle, as now 'restored' is glaring enough to discourage further excursion in that direction. Vulgar modern ecclesiastical small wares hideously out of place: the beautiful ancient carved seats crucified against the walls or against appalling stacks of hot water pipes slowly destroying them – their places usurped by vapid modern imitations.[4] What has been so handled is dead for ever, sacrificed on the cruel altar of modern folly.

I am yours faithfully
Larner Sugden

4   The 'vapid modern imitations' were presumably the oak seats given by the Revd John Maynard, the proposed removal of which caused such trouble in 1899 (see p. 85 below).

This has the whiff of a put-up job about it. Larner Sugden of Leek was a Socialist architect and friend of William Morris. He was one of the founder members of the SPAB and by 1892 was a committee member. Perhaps he was hoping to foment the sort of uproar that had greeted the proposed restoration of Blythburgh church a decade earlier (see p. 56 above). The SPAB's watchword to this day is 'repair', not 'restore', a view clearly spelled out in the letter, helpfully copied to the local press to make quite sure that it got further than the Revd Edward Scott's waste paper basket.

There is no record of any response or further controversy, but Mr Sugden's aspersions on the attempt to make the south aisle a worthy temporary place of worship while the restoration work was carried out (as seen in the photograph on p. 57), and in particular his characterization of the items so recently purchased as memorials to the rector's father as 'vulgar modern ecclesiastical smallware', must, one feels, have been hurtful.

There is quite a detailed description of the boarded-off portion of the church, which so charmed Larner Sugden, in a little guide book entitled *Round Aldeburgh* by C. R. B. Barrett,[5] published in 1892:

> Orford church . . . is interesting, though very ruinous.
>
> Within the church there is much cause for sorrow as to its condition. So unsafe has the roof of the nave and the north aisle become that it has been needful to board off the south aisle to be used for service, while the remainder of the church is deserted. On the floor of the north aisle, near the west end, rest the bells, which for years have never been hung up. Higher up, nearer the east end of the same aisle, the old seats of the Orford Corporation are dusty and disused. A few brasses, which by the way are carefully and wisely protected by wooden trapdoors, are to be found in the flooring . . . The organ, large, but much out of repair, may be crushed by the falling roof at any time. The east end, terminating where the chancel should begin, is a picture of desolation. Matters, however, are not going to remain in this condition (so I was informed) but subscription to a considerable amount are needed, and outside help ought to be forthcoming.

Then the author mentions one of the as-yet-unsolved mysteries of the interior of Orford church, the piscina (and a niche) at the west end of the south wall which, instead of being at waist height so that it could be used for its original function of providing a place for the ceremonial washing of the priest's hands and the vessels used for the Mass, is very close to ground level. He speculates that the floor of the south

---

5 *Barrett's Illustrated Guides: Suffolk Coast No. 2, Aldeburgh, Leiston, Orford, Butley*, Lawrence & Bullen, 1892, pp. 27–30.

Interior of Orford church, 1885,
watercolour paiting by Emmeline Rope

Communion plate made by Boulton & Fothergill, 1773

aisle must at some time have been raised considerably, and indeed this may have happened, perhaps after the archdeacon's visitation found in 1686 that the floor of the south aisle was 'sunk' (see p. 15 above). C. R. B. Barrett, like Larner Sugden, also spotted a 'beautiful ancient carved seat' and said, 'The poppy head on the old bench end near [the piscina and niche] is quaint and quite worth sketching.' Today the 'ancient' bench is placed against the south wall. Its ends do not match, one is a poppy head incorporating a grotesque face, the other, the one shown in the sketch, has panelled carving and a sort of roundel. Another single medieval poppy head bench end has been placed on loan to Orford Museum.

Poppy head bench end, piscina and niche

8

The First Phase – The Nave and North Aisle

Application was made to a grant-giving body, the Incorporated Church Building Society (ICBS). The Society had been founded in 1818 to provide funds for the building and enlargement of Anglican churches in England and Wales and was the foremost grant-giving body throughout the nineteenth century when there was so much church restoration and church building going on. The Society's work has, since 1982, been carried on by the Historic Churches Preservation Trust.

All the Society's records are now deposited in the library at Lambeth Palace, where the files relating to the Orford restoration may be read.[1]

The form applying for funds for the 're-seating and repairing' of St Bartholomew's is dated 22 November 1894. It gives a good picture of the church and the village. The population of Orford is given as 1,034 in 1891. Of those, 800 are described as 'poorer inhabitants' and the occupation of the chief portion of them is 'agricultural'. The present state of the church is described as 'very bad'. The amounts of money needed (£10,000) and raised so far (£1,300) are given. The endowments of the church are tithes 'at present under £230'. In reply to specific printed questions, assurances were given that there was a lightning conductor and that 'fixed kneeling boards' would be provided.

The ICBS was very fussy about seating. It particularly disliked the box pews which by the middle of the nineteenth century were to be found in most churches. Such pews were frequently constructed in a piecemeal manner, often occupied the centre of the church and were usually rented by the better-off families, leaving the humbler people to perch on cramped and uncomfortable benches at the sides. The design of the enclosed pews made kneeling difficult and in square pews not everyone could kneel facing the altar. The ICBS was keen to see the clutter of old pews cleared away, so grants were made only when extra seats were to be provided. The seats were to be free, and there was to be sufficient room between the rows for the worshippers to kneel down facing east.[2]

Because of this requirement, the existing seating arrangements in Orford church

---

1   ICBS files on St Bartholomew's church, Orford: 1226 (1830), 9830 (1894–1897), 10076 (1898–1902), Lambeth Palace Library.
2   *'A Church as it should be', the Cambridge Camden Society and its influence*, C. Webster & J. Elliott (eds), Shaun Tyas, 2000, p. 244.

in 1894 were described in great detail on the application form but did not, unfortunately, specify which were the medieval benches spotted by Mr Sugden and Mr Barrett (see pp. 61 and 65 above) and which were the box pews which can be seen in Emmeline Rope's picture (p. 63 above).[3] There were details of the west gallery, a free-standing structure 21 feet (6.5 metres) deep, positioned in front of the tower arch, which accommodated the organ as well as seats for thirty-four (which were quite possibly intended for the use of the choir), but all were said to be unusable because the gallery was 'ruinous'.

The total seating capacity of the church was 473. Emmeline Rope's picture shows just the first two or three rows of the pews in the nave. They are certainly of the box type, but they are not, apart possibly from the front pew which is painted red inside, square, and they seem to be of fairly uniform appearance. All had to be swept away.

The font in its former central position showing part
of the west gallery supported by props

3   In the nave, '23 pews or seats for adults 7' 6" in length each accommodating four people = 92, three pews or seats 14' 6" long accommodating nine = 27 [these, perhaps, were the medieval benches], odd pews or seats holding about 18. In the north aisle 56 seats.' All these are said to be unusable because of the ruinous state of the nave and aisle. In the south aisle '15 pews of 9' long held five each = 75, plus 171 chairs, making 246' – the only places available at that time out of a possible 473.

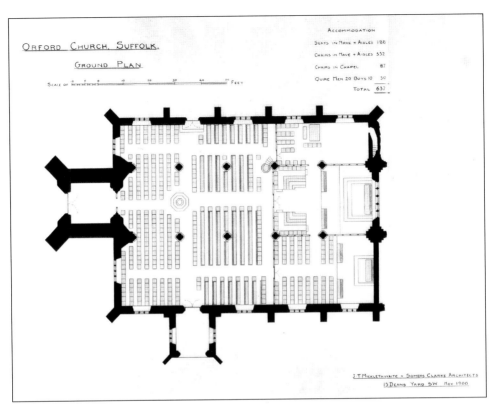

ACCOMMODATION

Seats in Nave + Aisles	188
Chairs in Nave + Aisles	532
Chairs in Chapel	87
Quire Men 20 Boys 10	30
TOTAL	637

ORFORD CHURCH, SUFFOLK.

GROUND PLAN

SCALE OF .... FEET

J T MICKLETHWAITE + SOMERS CLARKE ARCHITECTS
15 DEANS YARD SW Nov 1900

Seating plan for Orford church by J. T. Micklethwaite

The new scheme, shown on a plan attached to the application to the ICBS, was for an ambitious total of 615 seats to be provided in a mixture of fixed benches and chairs. This was almost certainly a gross over-provision. The Register of Services for 1898 to 1910 records a Sunday attendance of about a dozen communicants at the 8 a.m. service, with a number of the early services being abandoned through lack of a congregation, and not many more communicants at the 10.30 a.m. service. There was also an Evensong at 6.30 p.m. every Sunday. Although the total number of the congregation was not recorded, it is fair to guess that it was well under one hundred.[4]

In reply to the question 'What support have you or has your parish rendered to the Society in the last 10 years?' Edward Scott wrote, 'None that I know of', and the form was sent off.

Scarcely a week later he wrote to the Society urging a visit to Orford. 'The best trains from Liverpool Street are 11.50 a.m. and 3.20 p.m. We are eight miles from the station [Wickham Market] so the return journey on the same day is out of the

4 Register of Services 1898–1910, SRO(I) FC 168/C5/1.

question. I shall be glad to put you up.' The reply on 3 December came from the secretary to the Society, the Revd Ralph Milburn Blakiston:[5]

> I can come on Thursday next by the 3.20 train. That would enable me to accept your offer of hospitality for the night and to see the church etc by daylight on Friday. The church appears to be a very fine fabric. Apparently you do not contemplate the rebuilding of the Chancel at present.

The two men hit it off and the visit was obviously a success. The ICBS Orford file is endorsed '[£]80 for 1st portion. £40 paid February 1896. Balance £40. July 1896 Balance of £40 cancelled and a new grant of £100 made – (£40 paid Feb 1896). Balance £60 paid December 1897.'

Having secured the support of the ICBS, in April 1895 the Restoration Committee asked the architect 'to obtain tenders for the first section of the work, viz the main roof'. The minutes do not reveal how much money had been collected or promised by that date, but it is unlikely that it was far short of the £4000 which had been deemed necessary. On 20 May 1895 'Messrs Cornish & Gaymer's [of North Walsham] tender of £1795.7.0 was submitted to the committee by the chairman which included . . . repairing the east end and east window.' The tender was accepted.

In fact the east end and east window were not just 'repaired'. The altar was raised on four steps instead of two and the window was completely replaced and repositioned higher up in the lofty east end. It is tempting to wonder whether this unusual arrangement wasn't part of a scheme to furnish the east wall with a high 'gothic' reredos and that perhaps it was hoped that Lady Wallace could have been persuaded to give one of the pictures in her collection. There is, however, absolutely no evidence that Lady Wallace gave anything at all towards the restoration of Orford church. This is not to imply that she took no interest in the Church. We have seen that she presented a Bible to Sudbourne church, and in 1886 she presented a handsome set of communion plate (which is still in use) to the Anglican church in Paris.[6] The fact of the matter is that there are very few religious paintings in the Hertford/

---

5 Most of the Revd Ralph Milburn Blakiston's career was spent in church administration. He was ordained in 1868 and was a curate in Plymouth until 1874. From 1875 to 1899 he was secretary to the ICBS, but he also served as honorary secretary to bodies such as The Archbishop of Canterbury's Mission to the Assyrian Christians and the Association for Furtherance of Christianity in Egypt, to name but a few. In 1899 he returned to pastoral work as Dean of Bocking and rector of Hadleigh in Suffolk (*Crockford's Clerical Directory*, 1909). See also n. 6 on p. 80 below.

6 The building of St George's church in the rue Auguste-Vacquerie in 1887–88 was masterminded and partly funded by Sir Richard Wallace. That church was demolished and replaced in the late 1970s. (Matthew Harrison, *An Anglican Adventure, The History of St George's Anglican Church, Paris*, 2005, pp. 37–41, 42).

Wallace collections. The 4th Marquis preferred 'pretty' and 'pleasing' subjects.[7]

There is a curious, and very intrusive, piece of new architecture at the exterior of the east end where two tall buttresses have been cut into the Norman chancel arcade to support the east wall. It is hard to disagree with a later churchwarden and historian of the church, R. A. Roberts, when, after quoting an admiring description of the chancel remains, he wrote:

> Except in one unlovely particular. When in 1896 the last restoration of the church took place the architect conceived it to be necessary to support the eastern wall with two flying buttresses, surely the ugliest in form that architect could devise, and so placed as to cut the Norman arches in two, thus sadly interfering with their pristine beauty. He being dead, and also those who might have stayed his hand, he and they are beyond rebuke; but this is an instance where 'The evil deeds of men live after them'.[8]

The next committee meeting in December agreed that 'the order be given to Messrs Cornish & Gaymer to clean down the arches and replaster the walls inside the church'. On 8 February 1896 it was decided to spend £40 on embellishing the panels in the new roof with carved oak bosses, an attractive device which appeared in G. E. Street's otherwise unused plans (see p. 51 above). On 11 February Edward Scott wrote to the Revd Milburn Blakiston almost skittishly, asking for more money and adding: 'How will July suit you to come to us to preach for your Society and eat potatoes on the beach'?[9]

By April, 'pointing the north side of the church' and the chairman's order 'for the north aisle roof and parapet' were authorized by the Restoration Committee. Although not specifically itemized, it was probably at that point of the work that the round clerestory windows on the north side were opened up. When Davy described the church in 1808 he noted that 'the nave is lighted on the S side by 4 small quatre-foil clerestory windows. Those on the N side are stopped up'[10] (see the left-hand photograph on p. 116 below).

At the May meeting of the committee prices were given:

1 Flooring		£345. 0.0
2 Windows		76. 0.0

7 See, eg, *The Hertford Mawson Letters* (ed. John Ingamells), Wallace Collection, 1981, pp. 57, 77, 97.
8 R. A. Roberts, *'Oreford-Nigh-the-Seas'*, Richard Clay, Bungay, 1935, p. 20.
9 ICBS file 9830, Lambeth Palace Library.
10 *Collection for the History of Suffolk by Hundreds and Parishes*, British Library Add MSS 19077–19113 (microfilm in SRO (I)).

3	Plastering	58. 0.0
4	Pointing	77. 6.6
5	Digging & draining	37. 0.0
	Tank	15. 0.0
6	Buttresses	47.15.0
7	Altar & rails	36.10.0
8	Roof N aisle	621. 0.0
9	Parapet	145. 0.0
10	Hot water warming	158. 0.0
		1616.11.6
11	Provision for extra work	100. 0.0
		1716.11.6

On 2 July 1896 Edward Scott wrote again to the ICBS in much more formal terms:

Dear Sir,

You were good enough to give us a grant for the reroofing of Orford Church and with other kind help we have been enabled to raise the whole amount. We are therefore encouraged to proceed with the completion of the Nave and North Aisle. The estimated cost of the new proposed work is £1100. This includes floorings, warming and general repairs to wall and windows and will make this part of the church available for Divine Service which it has not been for some years. The accommodation in chairs will be about 360 exclusive of the part which is reserved for chancel. When this part of the church is ready we shall move into it and proceed with the repair of the south aisle.

You will readily understand that raising money in so remote a parish is a very difficult matter and we shall be grateful if your society will kindly give us a further grant towards the work.

As we have seen, the result was a further £20. On 17 July he wrote to thank the Society and noted that the following day someone would be 'coming down to inspect'.[11]

On 15 September further work was approved by the Restoration Committee:

1	Rood screen	£25. 0.0
2	Choir stalls	24.10.0
3	North door steps	6. 0.0
4	Tower floor	18. 0.0

11 ICBS file 9830, Lambeth Palace Library.

Just before Christmas (on 22 December 1896) 'it was resolved that the west end of the church should be oak blocked for seating and the chairman was authorized to instruct the architect to have the work carried out without delay'. The demolition of the west gallery must have been included in this work. The architect was also to be asked to 'send in drawings and the estimated cost of a canopy to stop the down draught at the east end'.

On 1 December 1897 the architect's certificate for completion of the work was sent in to the ICBS and £60 was duly paid. On 7 December Edward Scott wrote asking that the customary tablet acknowledging the assistance of the Society which was a condition of the grant, should not be installed in the church until the work on the whole building had been finished.

What is slightly puzzling is that, in spite of the terrifically detailed plans submitted to the ICBS showing a seating scheme with a mix of pews and chairs, there does not in fact seem to have been the slightest attempt to instal any pews at all in the nave and north aisle. Later generations have good reason to be delighted that the whole church, apart from the St Nicholas chapel and choir stalls, can be cleared and the chairs arranged in whatever configuration is wanted, which gives great flexibility.

Benjamin Britten at *Noye's Fludde* in Orford church, 1958. The audience is seated facing the west end; the north door can be seen.

That flexibility has proved to be particularly useful when Orford church is used for concerts. The first performances of four of Benjamin Britten's small-scale operatic works – *Noye's Fludde* in 1958 (remembered by Kenneth Clark on p. 11 above), and the three Church Parables, *Curlew River* in 1964, *The Burning Fiery Furnace* in 1966 and *The Prodigal Son* in 1968 – were all given in Orford church during the Aldeburgh Festival. These landmarks in twentieth-century music are commemorated on a slate roundel set into the floor of the nave in front of the tower arch.

After December 1896 there is an eighteen-month gap in the minutes of the Restoration Committee. This apparent lull (during which, of course, all the work to complete the nave and north aisle was being done) saw significant events in the lives of the members of the Scott family.

9

An Enormous Inheritance and the Second Phase –
The South Aisle

The first, doubtless welcome, development was the birth of a fifth child, a son, to Edward and Ida Scott. He was baptized Alexander Malcolm in Orford church on 7 February 1897.

Just nine days later, on 16 February, Lady Wallace died.

Under the terms of her will, the magnificent works of art kept on the ground and first floors of Hertford House were left to the nation and became the Wallace Collection. She left £100,000 to various charities and a similar amount in legacies, but it was John Murray Scott who inherited the whole of the rest of her enormous fortune, the lease on Hertford House, the estates in Ireland, Bagatelle and the apartment at 2 rue Lafitte in Paris. The contents of all the properties (especially those in Paris) were almost as magnificent as those in Hertford House, and they belonged to him alone.

What does seem rather shocking is Lady Wallace's favouring of John Murray Scott over her four grandchildren in France, even if she had no time for their mother, the actress. She was presumably following the instructions of her husband, and merely left them the freehold of a house in Paris which had been purchased by Richard Wallace in 1857.[1] As Lady Wallace, the former shop assistant, had lived in an unmarried state with Richard Wallace for thirty years, during which time she bore him a son, sayings about pots and kettles spring to mind. No one knows the true story, however. Perhaps Amélie-Suzanne Gall was already married when she started her liaison with Edmond Wallace (Bessie Scott said that 'they could not marry', see p. 45 above). There is also, of course, an outside chance that Lady Wallace might have made some provision for the children during her lifetime. Such was her generosity to her secretary that a number of contemporary newspaper reports stated that John Murray Scott was Sir Richard and Lady Wallace's adopted son.[2] This was not so.

---

1 Peter Hughes, *The Founders of the Wallace Collection*, Wallace Collection, 1981, p. 57. Sir Richard and Lady Wallace's three grandsons served with distinction in the French army during the First World War. The eldest, George, eventually rose to the rank of general and was made an officer of the Legion of Honour. His brother Henry also received a decoration. The younger brother, Edmond, was killed in 1915. Their sister, Georgette, like so many French women of her generation, was unmarried: Bernard Falk, *'Old Q's' Daughter*, Hutchinson, 1937 (reprint by Cedric Chivers Ltd, 1970), p. 295.

2 See, e.g., *Daily Graphic*, 29 April 1913, p. 7, 'The late Sir John Scott was the adopted son of Sir Richard and Lady Wallace.'

Netherswell Manor, Stow-on-the-Wold

John Murray Scott was known by his nephews and nieces as Uncle Johnny. Rather in the manner of today's Lottery winners, he bought houses for his family and paid for their holidays. He restored and enlarged Netherswell Manor at Stow-on-the-Wold in Gloucestershire as a home for his youngest brother Walter and his two sisters; he bought a house in Newmarket, Murray Lodge, for Malcolm and a house in Godalming for Douglas. Edward was still at Orford rectory, but when he retired in 1901 he, too, occupied a fine house at Branksome, Dorset, which may also have been funded by his fortunate eldest brother (see p. 90 below). John Murray Scott regularly rented a house in Scotland where he, his mother, Walter and the sisters took holidays. Apart from that we do not know to what extent, if at all, there was a 'trickle-down' of any of the money to other members of the Scott family and whether any of that money was used to pay for the restoration work at Orford church.

The only items listed in the terriers as the gift of the multimillionaire John Murray Scott are the two oak standard candlesticks which are still in use and stand on the altar steps. They are handsome and serviceable, but not exactly lavish.

The true size of Edward Scott's personal contribution to the cost of the restoration of St Bartholomew's is not known because the account books for the project have not survived. There are sufficient references to his gifts and loans as well, for example, as the inscription around the inside of the church porch ('In the year 1900 this porch being ruinous & falling was repaired in memory of John Scott and Alicia Lucy his wife by their son rector of this parish. Thanks be to God.'), to make it quite clear that at least some of the work was paid for by the rector from his own pocket – it must have been an expensive undertaking and it would have required funding from somewhere.

It should be remembered, however, that by the time John Murray Scott inherited the Wallace fortune, the first phase of the restoration had in fact been completed.

In any event, the decision was made to press ahead with further restoration work at Orford.

In May 1898 a new application form had been sent in to the ICBS and a new file started.[3] A summary in the file states:

> This is a very fine church built in the fourteenth century. It consists of a nave and aisles, the south aisle being in area as large as the nave. A few years since the whole was in a very ruinous condition. In 1895 and 1896 the nave and north aisle were substantially repaired and new roofs of oak covered with lead were put to them. This work cost £3,731 and the Society granted £100 towards this portion of the undertaking. Since their repair the nave and north aisle have been used for services. It is now proposed to repair the south aisle which has been partitioned off for years and restore it to use. A grant is asked for this portion.

The rest of the form is pretty much as the one submitted in 1894 except that the state of repair of the south aisle is described as 'deplorable' and instead of fixed kneeling boards it is said that hassocks will be provided. The costs are given as £2,200, plus

One of the pair of oak standard candlesticks given by John Murray Scott

3   ICBS file 10076, Lambeth Palace Library.

Watercolour painting of Sudbourne church in the mid-nineteenth century

Sudbourne church after restoration

Sir John Murray Scott

Left Malcolm Scott's and Bessie Maynard's wedding group in the garden of Great House.
The two child bridesmaids are the rector's daughters, Kathleen and Brida.
Right Wedding invitation

'architect's commission £110, architect's travelling expenses £15, salary of clerk of works £60, total £2,385. Funds raised so far are £950 from subscriptions, and £85 for the value of old materials. The deficiency is £1,350.'

The ICBS again decided to be helpful and in June made a grant of £70. Edward Scott wrote to the committee to thank them. 'It is very difficult to gather money nowadays and their kind reply to my appeal is most cheering.'

As before, there were detailed questions from the ICBS about existing and proposed seating arrangements. For the south aisle the proposal was that 77 would be accommodated in pews[4] and 225 in chairs making total seating for 302.

On 25 June 1898 a meeting of the Church Restoration Committee was held at which estimates for the south aisle roof and parapet were accepted, the work to be commenced in summer the following year. This meant that the wedding of Malcolm Scott and Bessie Maynard could be held on 24 August 1898 when the church was free of workmen (see p. 44 above).

As far as we can tell, the whole restoration project seems to have gone so smoothly as to be almost too good to be true. We can only marvel at Edward Scott's determination and stamina in seeing it through.

---

4   This seems to imply that the existing pews would remain. The original grant application form of 1894 had said that the south aisle contained 15 pews which would hold 75 people (see n. 3 on p. 67) although the architect Mr Micklethwaite had recommended two years earlier that they should be replaced (see chapter 11, below).

The new pulpit (paid for by the rector's father-in-law, George Fenwick) was dedicated on Thursday, 25 May 1899. The Archdeacon of Suffolk preached.[5] On 7 June 1899 Edward Scott wrote again to the Revd Milburn Blakiston (who had that year been appointed Dean of Bocking and rector of Hadleigh[6]). There seem for the first time to be signs that he was feeling the strain of the effort, and a hint that he was planning to retire:

> Don't think me a greedy brute: We have now begun the South Aisle and I want another £1000 to complete it. Do you think it would be any use my asking your good and kind Society to increase their promised grant of £70 to £100. I have now collected over £5000 and I can assure you it has been a hard struggle and my energy is nearly all expended. I am very anxious to complete the whole church bar the Tower this year and I am now making a special effort to get the £1000 necessary for the purpose. If I can accomplish this I shall be able to sing my Nunc Dim.[7] with greater ease.
>
> My curate has gone for his holiday. If the sun still shines on his return I will turn up at Hadleigh with coat, hat and Kodak.
>
> PS If this hot weather is on then I hae ma doots about the coat!!![8]

The reply he received dated 20 July said that consideration of his application would be deferred to the next year as all the money for the Norwich diocese had already been allocated. (Orford was at that time in the Norwich diocese; the diocese of St Edmundsbury & Ipswich was not created until 1914.)

Somehow from that moment things did not seem to go quite so well. Edward Scott, who seldom wrote any sort of comment in the Register of Services, noted by the entry for the evening service on 25 July 1899, 'v. poor congregation. Regatta night.' A few months later the south aisle seating was to cause a row. In fact there were much more serious troubles in the Scott family. The precipitating event was John Murray Scott's stupendous legacy from Lady Wallace.

---

5 Register of Services, 1898–1910, SRO(I) FC168/C5/1.
6 The parish of Hadleigh was a 'peculiar' of the Archbishop of Canterbury, meaning that it was outside the jurisdiction of the local bishop of Norwich. The Archbishop's Peculiar Deanery of Bocking consisted of the parishes of Moulton, Monks Eleigh and Hadleigh (Joanna Martin, 'Ecclesiastical Jurisdictions', *An Historical Atlas of Suffolk* (edited by David Dymond and Edward Martin), Suffolk County Council, 3rd edn, revised and enlarged 1999, pp. 24, 192). Presumably the Revd Blakiston was appointed as rector of Hadleigh in recognition of his service on several of the Archbishop's committees and other bodies.
7 The *Nunc Dimittis*, said or sung at Evensong: 'Lord, now lettest thou thy servant depart in peace', from St Luke's Gospel, chapter 2, verses 29–32.
8 ICBS file 10076, Lambeth Palace Library.

Mrs Sackville-West

John Murray Scott was a member of the committee set up by the government to mastermind the establishment of the Wallace Collection and remained a trustee until his death.[1] He was created a baronet for his efforts in 1899 and he took as his title Scott of Castle House, the name of the property in Lisburn, county Antrim which had formed part of his Wallace inheritance.[2]

Although Sir Richard Wallace had formed the intention during his lifetime of leaving his collection to the nation,[3] by the time the plan had been executed, Sir John Murray Scott was being credited in some quarters not only with supervising the operation but also with having secured the gift in the first place. An adulatory profile in *Vanity Fair* dated 14 April 1909 (complete with a genial portrait, see p. 78) states:

> First of all . . . he is a collector of *objets d'art*; and it is to him the nation owes the magnificent Wallace Collection, in Manchester Square. It is no longer a secret that this collection was offered to him by Lady Wallace, but, at his suggestion, was bequeathed by her to the English nation, and found a permanent home in London.

The article does not mention, of course, that Sir John's handsome fortune from the remainder of Lady Wallace's property was augmented to the tune of an additional £35,000 (just over £2 million today) when the government bought the remainder of his lease on Hertford House, which was then adapted so that it could house the collection for public display.[4]

The Wallace Collection was opened to the public on 22 June 1900 by Sir Richard Wallace's old friend, the Prince of Wales.

One of the very first groups of visitors to have a preview of the collection in March 1897, soon after Lady Wallace's death, included a remarkable woman, Mrs Victoria Sackville-West.

1 Peter Hughes, *The Founders of the Wallace Collection*, Wallace Collection, 1981, p. 58.
2 *Burke's Peerage and Baronetage*, 1912, 'Scott of Castle House'.
3 *The Founders of the Wallace Collection*, p. 54.
4 *Evening Standard*, 24 June 1913, '£1,000,000 Will', subheading 'Left to Sir John', transcript in Wallace Collection Archive, file 38.

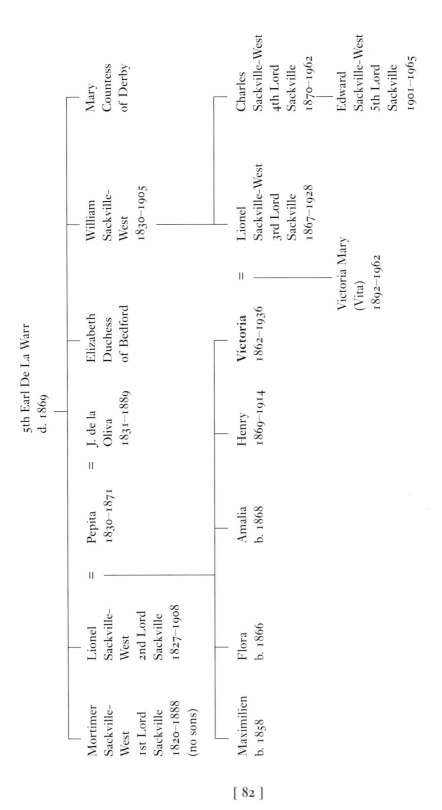

5th Earl De La Warr
d. 1869

Mortimer Sackville-West
1st Lord Sackville
1820–1888
(no sons)

Lionel Sackville-West
2nd Lord Sackville
1827–1908

=

Pepita
1830–1871

=

J. de la Oliva
1831–1889

Elizabeth Duchess of Bedford

William Sackville-West
1830–1905

Mary Countess of Derby

Maximilien
b. 1858

Flora
b. 1866

Amalia
b. 1868

Henry
1869–1914

Victoria
1862–1936

=

Lionel Sackville-West
3rd Lord Sackville
1867–1928

Charles Sackville-West
4th Lord Sackville
1870–1962

Victoria Mary (Vita)
1892–1962

Edward Sackville-West
5th Lord Sackville
1901–1965

Sackville family tree

She was one of the five illegitimate children of the 2nd Lord Sackville (of Knole in Sevenoaks, Kent, a beautiful, rambling and ancient house now in the care of the National Trust) and a Spanish dancer called Pepita. Victoria had been brought up in France but was received into the Sackville family circle when she was eighteen and lived with her father at Knole. She leap-frogged the twin bars to her inheritance of the Sackville title and property (her illegitimacy and the fact that she had brothers) by marrying her cousin, Lionel Sackville-West, who was the heir. In 1892 they had a daughter, Vita (Vita Sackville-West, poet, writer and gardener who created Sissing-hurst Castle gardens in Kent, now also owned by the National Trust). Life was not plain sailing for Victoria. The costs of the upkeep of Knole were ruinous and the property was heavily mortgaged. After a happy start, her marriage began to fall apart and her husband was having affairs with other women. Her meeting with the fabulously wealthy bachelor John Murray Scott in 1897 gave her a whole new project to pursue.[5]

After Sir John sold the lease of Hertford House to the government, he moved into a property at 5 Connaught Place and he furnished it with some of the many items which he had inherited. One wonders whether there wasn't a slightly mischievous motive in his choice of Connaught Place, the very street where in 1871 the 5th Marquis of Hertford had set up home in his 'Hertford House' after he had sold the lease of Hertford House in Manchester Square to Sir Richard Wallace (see p. 32 above).

Although 5 Connaught Place was also Mrs Scott's home, by the end of 1899 Mrs Sackville-West was acting as hostess there. The Sackvilles called Sir John Seery.[6] Vita, whom he called Kidlet, was a frequent visitor. Scott was infatuated. His family were appalled.

It seems that Mrs Sackville-West deliberately set out to cause trouble between Sir John and his family:

> She began by humiliating them in the guise of helpfulness. She rearranged the furniture in their houses; she asked her own friends to Seery's dinner-parties 'to make them more lively'; she then suggested that only one sister at a time, and later none, need attend these parties, 'for people don't come to meet your sisters'.[7]

The tactic worked, because for their part, the Scotts did their best to avoid her. Malcolm always asked, when he received an invitation to dinner, whether Mrs Sackville-West would be there. If she was to attend, he and his wife stayed away.[8]

5   Victoria Glendinning, *Vita, The Life of V. Sackville-West*, Weidenfeld & Nicolson, 1983, pp. 17–18.
6   The seven-year-old Vita Sackville-West called John Murray Scott Seery because she heard his French servants call him 'Seer John'. Ibid., p. 20.
7   Nigel Nicolson, *Portrait of a Marriage*, Weidenfeld & Nicolson, 1973, p. 68.
8   Information from Nigel Sheffield, Malcolm Scott's grandson.

Victoria Sackville-West and Vita, 1899

Victoria was particularly anxious to thwart Sir John's plan to make Walter, the youngest brother, his secretary. She pretended that Walter had fallen in love with her and told Sir John that his brother was making advances to her, knowing that it would make him jealous. Walter, who found the whole thing preposterous, went to see her and asked her to desist from making mischief. He then had a heart-to-heart with Sir John at 5 Connaught Place, pointing out the damage that the friendship was doing to the family. Their mother overheard the conversation, was deeply upset, rushed to her room, had a heart attack and died the following day, 17 November.[9]

Mrs Alicia Lucy Scott was buried in Orford churchyard on 21 November 1899. She was clearly much loved by her children. She had married their father when she was only sixteen years old and had been seventeen when John Murray Scott was born. There can be little doubt that in their grief, most of the Scotts felt that it was Mrs Sackville-West who had been responsible for their mother's death.

9 These events were recounted during the later legal proceedings concerning John Murray Scott's will: *Evening Standard*, 24 June 1913, see n. 4 above.

The Affair of the Pews and the Rector's Departure

Edward Scott was unable to attend the meeting of the Church Restoration Committee on 18 November 1899 because of the death of his mother but the meeting was held and, having 'expressed their regret for the cause which prevented the rector from being present and desired the Secretary to write a letter conveying their sincere sympathy and condolence with him in his bereavement', it resolved to 'proceed with the plastering'. More significantly, 'it was also resolved that a reserve of £2 be put on each of the benches to be sold on Monday next' (20 November). At the next meeting on 9 December 'some discussion took place as to the re-purchase of the benches which were sold by auction on 20 November'. It was decided to consult the architect, Mr Micklethwaite, before making a decision.

On 29 December Mr Micklethwaite himself attended a committee meeting. The minutes, much more extensive than any others in the book, are in Edward Scott's handwriting, because the secretary, Walter Rope, had resigned. A petition dated 13 December was handed in and was read:

> To the rector and churchwardens of Orford
> We the undersigned parishioners of Orford viewed with deep regret the sale of the benches in the church which were the gift of the late and much respected rector the Rev. John Maynard. Hearing that Mr. Crisp who purchased them is willing to resell them to the Church Restoration Committee for the price he gave for them we therefore earnestly beg you to consider his offer and if possible buy them back and give them some place in the church.

The petition was signed by thirty-one people, Walter Rope, the erstwhile secretary, being the first signatory. Edward Scott told the committee that although he backed the decision to get rid of the benches, he did not feel able to take any decision on the petition, and that his curate, the Revd P. H. Osmond, by then a member of the committee, should not vote on it either. Mr Micklethwaite's opinion was sought, and he quoted from his report written back in 1892:

> There is a block of oak seats in the south aisle which show very good intentions on the part of those who put them there and in a general view of the church

The south aisle after restoration and without the pews. Compare its orderly appearance with the photograph on p. 57 above.

these pews look very well. Unfortunately they are not of a good section and are not comfortable either for sitting or kneeling and the ends are not made . . . as they should be and are already beginning to come to pieces. It would be possible to work them up into a better form but it will be much better to have all new.

He urged the committee to stick to their guns. The hapless three remaining decision-takers 'after long discussion' bravely resolved not to buy back the benches, but said that they might remain in the church until it was necessary to remove them for the reflooring of the south aisle.

At the next meeting, on 13 January 1900, Walter Rope was elected back on to the committee and Edward Scott showed what he was made of. He 'expressed his desire to see the south aisle of the church completed', thereby accelerating the demise of the Maynard pews,[1] and volunteered to 'advance the sum of £300 [about £18,000 in

1 Although according to R. A. Roberts, see p. 121 below, they were put back in 1914, whether 'worked up into a better form' or not, we do not know. There are ten pews in the St Nicholas chapel today, five on each side, and each block of five is in a different style, one set with poppy heads and the other without. The 1922 terrier, very detailed in most respects, even listing the 'rearrangement of

The nave after restoration. Note the plain temporary rood screen, the clear glass
in the east window and the font still in the centre of the church.

today's money] without interest for this purpose'. Estimates of £138 1s 7d for reflooring the south aisle without the oak blocks and £47 for screens for the north and south aisles (see p. 108 below) were also accepted. Mr Micklethwaite was to be instructed to obtain estimates for the oak block flooring and the completion of the heating and to carry on the work of the south aisle to its completion.

In February the new secretary of the ICBS, obviously preparing to reconsider the grant application, wrote to enquire how much money had been raised and whether the sums of money in the 1898 form still held good. The reply dated 24 February said that only £500 remained to be found and that if the £70 promised by the ICBS and £25 promised from the Diocesan Building Society were taken into account, the balance was £400. The file bears the note, '[£]20 add[itional] in all [£]90.' On 16 March Edward Scott wrote a letter of thanks for the extra £20. The task of raising the final few hundred pounds was very hard. The churchwardens' accounts show among the receipts for 1900: 'June 16. Jumble Sale (Rev. E. M. Scott) £12 0 0.'[2]

---

curtain hangings to the altar', is entirely silent on what must still have been the sensitive subject of the pews.

2 Churchwardens' Book containing disbursements 1866–1920, SRO(I) FC168/E5/2. This is an early use of the word 'jumble sale'. The first example cited in *The Oxford English Dictionary* is from 1898.

The service for the opening of the south aisle after the restoration was held on St Bartholomew's Day, 24 August 1900. Edward Scott wrote in the Register of Services, 'All now complete.'[3]

He wrote once more to the ICBS on 12 November 1900 to ask if they could make the promised £90 up to £100. He pointed out that the amount raised and spent on Orford church was very near £7000. The letter sent by return of post was not a friendly one: 'I am bound to tell you that the Committee have dealt with your case in an *unusually* liberal manner already.' On 16 November Edward Scott simply wrote a letter of thanks for the £90. It is the last of his letters in the ICBS file.

Thereafter, the recorded activities of the Restoration Committee also peter out. We know that the south porch was restored in 1900, but there is no record of that work apart from the inscription on the beams. There was one more routine meeting on 18 January 1901. It was resolved that the treasurer be empowered to pay various bills for repairs to the roof and new shed: W. Chapman £7 19 3 and Mr Gibbs £35 10 6 and the rector £11 10 3 (the only recorded payment to him). Votes of thanks were passed for the chairman and treasurer.

Six days later Edward Scott resigned the living, aged fifty-one, having been rector for twenty-four years, and perhaps wondering whether his memory would be as fiercely defended by the Orford parishioners as was that of his predecessor, John Maynard.

On Sunday, 13 January 1901, he had written in the Register of Services, 'My last Sunday as Rector.' In fact he took the services on two more Sundays and the feast of the Conversion of St Paul (25 January). He went out with a bang, as it happened. On Sunday, 27 January, he wrote, 'Special Services with reference to the death of Queen Victoria. My last Sunday at Orford. E.M.S.' The Queen had died on 22 January. It was indeed the end of an era.

We can only admire Edward Scott's single-mindedness. When the Suffolk historian Vincent Redstone was beginning to investigate the history of Orford, he contacted the rector to see if he could shed any light on the relationship between the church of Sudbourne and its chapel-of-ease at Orford. When Edward Scott replied he must have asked Vincent Redstone to give a 'plug' for the restoration project, and Redstone duly obliged in the first article about Orford that he wrote for the *Proceedings of the Suffolk Institute of Archaeology*:

> A great work of judicious preservation and restoration has been recently under-
> taken by the Rev. E. M. Scott, acting under the directions of the well-known
> architect, Mr. Micklethwaite, FSA, who estimates that an expenditure of

3 Register of Services, 1898–1910, SRO(I) FC168/C5/1.

£10,000 will be necessary to place the church in a fit condition for Divine Service. The Rector writes:

'I am now doing all I can to get the South Aisle restored. This will cost £2,500, of which I have collected £1,100. I hope you will mention this and urge your members to help me in this matter, and also get their friends to take an interest in this great work.'[4]

In answer to Redstone's question about the origins of Orford church, Edward Scott sent the following, almost certainly erroneous, note: 'The chancel was part of a monastery chapel, the nave and centre tower of which were pulled down in the early part of the 14th century, and replaced by the present church . . .' Redstone reproduced the note in his article, albeit in quotation marks, and it has found its way into a number of other books since.[5]

A tribute is to be found in the Editor's Note to a little book published in 1911 by the English Monumental Inscriptions Society:

A former Rector of Orford (the Rev. Edward Maude Scott), to whom is chiefly due the admirable restoration of the church there, merits special mention here for the wise measures he adopted (1877–1900) for the preservation of the Brasses.[6]

4   Vincent Burrough Redstone,'The Sandling, III Orford', *Proceedings of the Suffolk Institute of Archaeology*, vol. X (1897–98), pp. 89, 96.

5   Orford's 'monastery', a house of Augustinian friars, was established in 1295 (grant of land in Orford by Robert de Hewell to the Augustinian friars of London, 23 Edward I, Public Record Office, C 43/24/11), rather more than a hundred years *after* the Norman church with its chancel, nave and central tower had been built. While it was not unknown for religious communities to take over part of a parish church (for example the Benedictine nuns at Bungay used the chancel of St Mary's church in the town, leaving only the nave for the parishioners), the friary in Broad Street in Orford had its own chapel. At least two wills of Orford citizens make the distinction between the friary chapel and the parish church quite plain. Sir Henry Wingfield in 1493 (P.C.C. Vox. 29, printed in *Suffolk Wills (Orford)*, note 6, below) specified that he wished to be 'buried in the chancel before the high altar in the Freres (i.e. friary) of Orford . . . I give to the high altar of the parish church . . . 13s and 4d and 20s . . .'. John Freer in 1520 (Norwich Consistory Court will registers, vol. 49) asked 'to be buried in the chapel of Our Lady within the parish church of Orford'. He left sums for various purposes to St Bartholomew's, then he left to the Austin Friars for the reparation of '*their church*', 20 shillings.

    Vincent Redstone was just dipping his toe into the water of Orford's history when his article was published. His final sentence was: 'This paper is but a short sketch of part of the town's history, there yet remains to be written a history worthy of this old and ancient borough', and indeed he went on to undertake much more research and to publish further articles which are most illuminating, e.g. 'Orford and its Castle', *Proceedings of the Suffolk Institute of Archaeology*, vol. X, pp. 205–30; 'The Suffolk Shore' in *Memorials of Old Suffolk*, Bemrose & Sons, 1908, pp. 221–41.

6   *Suffolk Wills (Orford) proved in the Prerogative Court of Canterbury Between 1383 and 1800*, compiled by H. W. B. W[ayman], Poole and Pemberton for the English Monumental Inscriptions Society, 1915.

Birkdale, Branksome Park, unchanged from the time that Edward Scott and his family lived there, apart from the building on the extreme right which is a chapel built for the later occupants, the Carmelite nuns

Edward and Ida Scott and their family moved to Branksome near Bournemouth where Ida Scott's parents lived. 'Birkdale', the family's substantial and handsome house, stood in ten acres in the exclusive residential development of Branksome Park.[7] There was a staff cottage in the grounds and at that time it would have been possible to walk from the garden of Birkdale through woods to the beach at Branksome Chine, a facility doubtless appreciated by the four young Scott children, still aged only thirteen, ten, eight and four. Edward Scott did not take on another parish but from 1910 he served as curate of All Saints' Church, built in 1875 at the centre of the estate by the owner and developer of Branksome Park.[8]

The last word on Edward Scott's achievement should be that of the Bishop of St Edmundsbury & Ipswich as reported in the *Suffolk Chronicle and Mercury* in 1921 at

7 'Birkdale' was a Carmelite nunnery from 1927 to 1992 and is now part of the Victoria Education Centre for physically disabled students (information from Mrs Hazel Vallier, a teacher at the school).

8 *Kelly's Directory* for Bournemouth, Dorset, 1911 & 1915, and church guide to All Saints' Church, Branksome Park.

the service of dedication of the new rood screen and choir stalls erected by his widow (see p. 108 below):

> . . . Edward Maude Scott was the man to whom, more than any other single man, [the parishioners] owed the renewed glory of one of the noblest churches in Suffolk. His faith, his perseverance, his zeal, his love of beauty in the service of God, prevailed over all the inevitable difficulties of so great an undertaking. . . . that building, to which he had given new life and new permanence, was in itself the outward and visible sign of his spirit, which was now enshrined in the screen and the stalls.[9]

9 *Suffolk Chronicle and Mercury*, 4 November 1921, 'Orford Memorials Dedicated'.

12

Church Furnishings

No terrier seems to have been compiled during the 'restoration years' of 1894 to 1902. The supplemental terrier of 1902 is therefore particularly interesting because it shows that the restoration of the church building was accompanied by an internal reordering and redecoration, much of it funded by members of the Scott family, although other members of the community also contributed. The items added were:

A brass altar cross inlaid with oxidized silver and a pair of brass candlesticks,
with imitation candles and oil burners, presented by the Revd and Mrs
P. H. Osmund [the curate and his wife]

Brass eagle lectern in side chapel presented by the Misses Scott and
Walter M. Scott Esq.

Processional cross the gift of D. M. Scott Esq.

Brass candelabra presented by Mrs Scott

Brass hanging lamp given by H. N. Baron Esq. [the new doctor]

Carved oak pulpit on stone base the gift of George Fenwick Esq.
[Mrs Ida Scott's father]

Oak altar

Oak credence table with black marble top

Two long oak kneeling desks for communicants in lieu of rails

One oak fald stool¹ in memory of Phyllis Maud Scott

Two oak standard candlesticks given by J. M. Scott Esq.

Large oak altar frontal chest

Two banners presented by the Revd and Mrs P. H. Osmund

Turkey carpet in sanctuary given by T. Lloyd Place Esq.
[the previous doctor and committee member]

Axminster carpet in side chapel sanctuary the gift of Mr and Mrs D. M. Scott

Long velvet pile kneeling strip

---

1   Strictly speaking, a stool with folding legs placed to the north of the altar in the sanctuary for use of
a bishop in place of a throne. The term is also applied to a litany desk or prie-dieu, which is what
we have in Orford church, given in memory of the rector's baby twin daughter who had died just as
the restoration campaign was started, see p. 59 above.

Two pairs of blue hangings

Two red velveteen dossals,[2] one in side chapel given by T. L. Place Esq.

Red printed felt hanging for vestry

Standard lamp in churchyard

Building in churchyard 14 feet by 9 feet . . . galvanised iron sides and roof
    [the sexton's shed]

Almost all of these things are still giving good service, and members of the congregation (especially the volunteers who make up the church cleaning parties) will recognize them. At least one item can also be identified in the Jones & Willis catalogue of 1899. The brass eagle lectern still in the side (now St Nicholas) chapel is a copy of a medieval lectern found in the lake at Newstead Abbey in Nottinghamshire (into

The side (now St Nicholas) chapel lectern

2   Fabric hung as a screen on the wall behind an altar in place of a reredos.

which, presumably, it had been thrown at the Reformation) and now in Southwell Minster. It cost £90. Turkey carpet similar to the one in the sanctuary was priced at 18s per square yard.

The Incorporated Church Building Society did not overlook the matter of the plaque recording their really rather modest contribution of £190 to the £7000 total cost of the work at Orford (see p. 72 above). A slightly frantic-sounding letter to the Society from F. J. B. Hart, the curate to the new rector, the Revd Frederick Anstruther Cardew,[3] dated 15 March 1902, assured the Society that the plaque had arrived and was in the church but asked whether he could delay getting it fixed in the porch until the rector, who was away sick, came back so that he could decide on its exact position.[4] There is no trace of it today.

It seems that Orford church had, prudently, begun to make regular contributions to ICBS. A list, recently found in the church, showing the good causes to which the church collections were to be given each month in 1900 shows that in July the money went to the Church Building Society. It is a guess that this had been the case each year since Dean Blakiston came to preach and to eat potatoes on the beach in July 1896.

The 1908 supplemental terrier shows that Edward Scott's generosity continued into his retirement:

A two manual organ
A green altar frontal & super frontal the gift of the Revd & Mrs Anstruther
    Cardew [the new rector]
White, green, red & violet frontals & superfrontals
Two oak prayer desks the gift of the Revd E. Maude Scott

---

3 The Revd F. A. Cardew had been born in India (his father Sir Frederick Cardew KCMG was later Governor of Sierra Leone). As a young man he travelled in Canada (fighting with the 91st Winnipeg Light Infantry in the North West Indian Rebellion), then went to the 'wild west' of the United States and to Mexico. He was ordained in 1891, was curate of Kensington from 1891 to 1894 but came to Sudbourne with Orford from Australia where he had been the rector of All Saints, Charville, Queensland from 1895 to 1897 and rector of All Saints, Brisbane from 1897 to 1900 (*Crockford's Clerical Directory*, 1903). He lasted seven years at Sudbourne with Orford before succumbing to wanderlust once more. In 1907 he went to Paris as Chaplain of St George's Anglican Church where he remained until 1934. He obtained that post through the influence of Sir John Murray Scott who, by virtue of his connection with Sir Richard and Lady Wallace and then his inheritance of their property, was well known and respected in Paris. (Information supplied by his son, Dr Peter Cardew, and from Matthew Harrison, *An Anglican Adventure, The History of St George's Anglican Church, Paris*, 2005, pp. 55–6.) The Revd F. A. Cardew undertook philanthropic activities in Paris, running a social centre and hostel attached to St George's for the many young English women (some of them girls barely into their teens) who came to the Paris theatres to work as dancers. The Cardew Club (as it became) survived until the 1990s, looking after au pair girls, students and young English-speaking foreigners (ibid., pp. 56–60, 84).

4 ICBS file 10076, Lambeth Palace Library.

Offertories.

1900.

Jan. 14	Life Boat
21	War Fund
Feb. 25	Diocesan Fund
Mar. 18	Society Propagation Christian Know.ᵉ
Apr. 15	Clergy Sustentation Fund
22	Lebombo Mission
May 20	Additional Curates Society
June 17	Society Propagation of Gospel
July 15	Church Building Society
29	East Suffolk Hospital
Aug. 19	Waifs and Strays
Sep. 16	Agricultural Benevolent Society
30	National Society
Oct.ʳ 21	Idiots' Asylum
Nov.ʳ 18	Society Propagation of Gospel
Dec.ʳ 16	Shipwrecked Mariners' Society
30	Church Army

List of 'Offertories' for 1900

An oak & brass bound chest, for the communion vessels the gift of Mr William
    Toller [who faithfully served on the restoration committee throughout
    its existence[5]]
One brass corona having six lamps
One bracket lamp
Two pairs of small brass flower vases

The 'coronas' recorded in the 1894 terrier as well as the second six-lamp one listed
above are almost certainly the rather handsome light fittings now adapted to electricity
and hanging in the east end of the church. They have been augmented by others with
eight lights in the nave.

5   See pp. 55 and 86 above.

13

Sir John Murray Scott's Will

Sir John Murray Scott's infatuation with Lady Sackville (her husband had become the 3rd Lord Sackville in 1908) went on.

What was the attraction? She was, by any standard, an impossible woman. Maybe Victoria's colourful background, not dissimilar to that of the women in the lives of his former employer, Sir Richard Wallace, the 4th Marquis of Hertford and the 3rd Marquis (Mie-Mie had also been the illegitimate daughter of a dancer), appealed to him.

Victoria was a volatile and demanding woman. She ran rings round Sir John. He was a great big softy, by all accounts. He was 6 foot 4 inches tall, he weighed 25 stone and was allegedly 60 inches round the waist. No one believes that his relationship with Victoria was a sexual one.[1] He was, however, soon giving her very large sums of money. He paid for a law suit brought by her brother. He bought her a house in Mayfair. It was estimated that he gave her £84,000 (nearly £5 million in today's money) while he was alive. He also told her that he intended to leave her £150,000 and all the art collection in his apartment in rue Lafitte in his will. Presumably it was her desire to conceal these gifts from his family that was the motivation for her spiteful attempts to prevent Walter Scott from becoming his brother's secretary (see p. 84 above).

Victoria and her daughter Vita, sometimes accompanied by her father (Lord Sackville) and her husband and his latest lady friend, visited Paris with Sir John, staying in his properties in the rue Lafitte or at Bagatelle (though he sold Bagatelle and disposed of its contents and the garden statuary in 1904). Vita described the rue Lafitte apartment:

> One could stand at one end of the apartment and look down a long vista of rooms opening into one another, with an unbroken stretch of shining parquet floor, and all the rooms were panelled with cream-white and gilt Louis XV *boiserie*, or else with faded old green silk. All the furniture was French, with rich ormolu mounts, and there were hanging chandeliers in every room, and sconces on the walls, and, in the big gallery, priceless Boucher tapestries.[2]

---

1   Nigel Nicolson, *Portrait of a Marriage*, Weidenfeld and Nicolson, 1973, pp. 21, 58.
2   Ibid., pp. 21–2.

Sir Richard Wallace's study at Hertford House, giving some idea of the splendour of John Murray Scott's inheritance

This gives some idea of what was *not* in the Wallace Collection. Although the superb pictures in Lord Hertford's collection had been moved to London, competition for wall space meant that it was not possible also to display the fine tapestries in Hertford House, so they remained in Paris. Again, probably for lack of space, an outstanding group of French eighteenth-century sculpture was kept at the rue Lafitte. There was furniture and porcelain equal in quality and quantity to that in the Wallace Collection.

Vita also tells us that the fortunate John Murray Scott slipped easily into a lifestyle which matched his resources:

Seery kept up a tremendous *train de maison* there; every flower, fruit and vegetable seemed to be out of season, and larger than they would have been anywhere else *in* season. But it wasn't in the least ostentatious; it all seemed perfectly fitting and natural.[3]

3 Ibid.

She casts an interesting light on Seery's[4] character and abilities (which perhaps makes one wonder about his competence as Sir Richard Wallace's secretary):

> He was the best humoured, most lovable, genial and generous man imaginable. Everybody loved him . . . Seery was always laughing, when he wasn't asleep – laughing, and saying 'Shoo!, pshoo!' to the swarm of flies that was for ever buzzing around his fat face in summer, and at which he used to flick perpetually with an enormous silk pocket-handkerchief. He prided himself on being a very good organiser, and very methodical, but as a matter of fact he muddled every arrangement, and mislaid all his possessions, in spite of the innumerable drawers and leather cases in which he used to put things away. When I think of Seery I see him sitting before an immense writing-table, rattling a bunch of keys and trying every key in every lock in turn . . . Then when he had got a drawer open, Mother would come and make a pounce at his stamps, and he would cry, 'Go away, you little beggar', or 'you little Spanish beggar', but of course he worshipped her and let her have what she wanted.[5]

It seems that Vita was sometimes 'parked' with Seery's mother and his two sisters when they were holidaying at the property, Sluie, in Scotland which he customarily rented. That was where she was in September 1908 when the news arrived of the death of her grandfather, which meant of course that her father became the 3rd Lord Sackville and her mother Lady Sackville. The picture she paints of Mary Scott is unkind and unflattering:

> One of Seery's sisters – the big one, whom her family called the Duchess[6] – came into my room before breakfast with the telegram; she had on a pink flannelette dressing gown, and no false hair, and I remember noticing how odd she looked. She kissed me in a conscientious sort of way, but I wasn't very much moved over Grandpapa's death just then; it only sank in afterwards . . . Then I went down to Seery's room, and never to my last moment shall I forget the sight he presented, sitting at his dressing-table perfectly oblivious, the twenty-five stone of him, dressed only in skin-tight Jaegar combinations, and, dear warm-hearted old Seery, crying quite openly over the telegram.[7]

4 See n. 6 to chapter 10 above.
5 *Portrait of a Marriage*, p. 20.
6 Mary was indeed big. She was unusually tall, see the frontispiece wedding photograph where she is standing next to John Murray Scott whom we know to have been 6' 4" tall, and the photo on p. 105.
7 *Portrait of a Marriage*, pp. 27–8.

Soon after Lord Sackville's death, Victoria's brother brought a law suit, trying to prove that his parents had been married and that he was the heir. He lost, but the legal fees amounted to £40,000, adding to the financial embarrassment of the Sackvilles. Seery helped out with loans that he soon converted into gifts. In the autumn of 1909 he took Victoria and Vita on an exciting and exotic holiday to Russia.

Vita did understand that her mother did not treat the generous Seery well. After witnessing a dreadful quarrel between them in 1910, she wrote:

> I thought they would quarrel for good, but he became apologetic and they have half patched it up, though it can't be as before. It was all very unpleasant, and they called each other names [we have already seen that one of Seery's names for Lady Sackville, meant affectionately, and certainly perceptive, was 'little beggar' or 'little Spanish beggar'], and I hated it . . . I am awfully sorry for Seery! After all, we were the only interest in his life, and he is old; he cried this afternoon.[8]

Seery's mother, brothers and sisters and their families would have been hurt to learn that, in the eyes of the Sackvilles, they were of no interest in his life.

Sir John Murray Scott was actually only sixty-three years old, but he was not in good health. Vita was just eighteen. She met an impecunious young diplomat, Harold Nicolson, and they fell in love, but marriage was thought to be out of the question, given what Lady Sackville considered to be the Sackville family's straitened circumstances. Seery very much disapproved of a business venture she had undertaken, declaring that she needed to make some money; it was an interior-decorating shop in South Audley Street in Mayfair. Ever conscious that Seery could alter his will and indeed frequently threatened to do so, she tried to keep on good terms with him, but her volatile temperament meant that her tongue often ran away with her. She obviously feared that she had overstepped the mark in October 1911 because she wrote to a friend, Mrs Cooke, saying that Sir John was making a new will by which the Sackvilles would get nothing. She was right to be uneasy. He got as far as drafting a codicil to his will revoking his legacies to Lady Sackville except for £20,000 and the income on £30,000, and leaving the bulk of his estate to his nephews and nieces. By January 1912 Seery and Victoria were back on speaking terms. They went together to Malcolm Scott's house at Newmarket on 13 January (see pp. 102, 103 below). On 16 January Seery called on Lady Sackville at her shop. She described the visit in her diary:

> He called upon me about the possibility of Vita marrying H.N. whom he likes

8 Victoria Glendinning, *Vita, The Life of V. Sackville-West*, Weidenfeld & Nicolson, 1983, p. 37.

Murray Lodge, Newmarket

enormously and he promised to give her . . . £100 per month. He also told me he would alter his will if I was not nice to him, and called me several times: *you little rascal* and went away on those words.[9]

On the following day Sir John Murray Scott suddenly died of a heart attack at Hertford House. His will had not been changed.

He was buried in Orford churchyard on 20 January. When the contents of the will and its five codicils were revealed the Scott family must have been appalled; they called the Sackvilles 'The Locusts'[10] even before they knew about the will. It was then that they took the decision which made them the talk of London society and gave the newspapers a field day. They decided to contest the will.

It was not a unanimous decision. It is thought that Malcolm was the driving force behind the case, probably supported by the 'Netherswell Three' – Mary, Alicia and Walter. The General, Douglas, was against it. Edward Scott's position is not known.[11]

9 Ibid., p. 43.
10 *Portrait of a Marriage*, p. 59.
11 Information supplied by Martin Cardew.

14

The Talk of the Town

The most astonishing thing about Sir John Murray Scott's will is the enormous size of the estate. It was valued at £1,180,000. In today's money that is over £66 million.

The will was dated 26 October 1900. Lady Sackville was left some important jewellery ('as souvenirs of a sincere friendship'), £150,000 and the pictures, furniture and works of art in the rue Lafitte apartment (valued at £350,000, 'in token of my gratitude for her goodness and sympathetic kindness to me at all times and more particularly on the occasion of the great sorrow of my life [his mother's death]'). How the Scotts must have ground their teeth. To rub salt in the wound, the French and English death duties payable were to come from the residue which was the part which the Scotts would be sharing. If one takes the bequests to Lady Sackville as being worth £550,000 and the duties to be 40 per cent, she would be taking £770,000 of the £1,180,000 and it must be remembered that she had relieved Sir John of £84,000 while he was still alive.

The will also gave money to various friends, relatives and servants and provided that the residue should be divided into hundredths and that 20 parts should go to Douglas, 15 parts each to Edward and Malcolm and 25 parts to Mary. Walter was given £10,000 and an annuity of £2,000 and the house and contents at 5 Connaught Place were left in trust to Mary and Alicia.

Of course, looked at rationally, the will still left about £400,000 for the Scotts, but rational thought seldom plays a part in that sort of situation.

The first of five codicils was dated 23 November 1908 and it diverted the most valuable items in 5 Connaught Place, worth about £50,000, to Lady Sackville and gave Lord Sackville £30,000. Sir John divided his own jewellery and guns amongst his brothers and made further pecuniary legacies to his servants and friends including Bessie Scott's brother, Dr John Maynard, who was given £1,000.

The first legal proceedings, in April 1912, involved the opening by a judge in the Probate court of a sealed envelope which had been enclosed in a letter from Sir John to Lady Sackville (addressed to '*ma chère petite amie*'). The letter had directed that the envelope should be opened only after his death, 'should there be any disposition shown to dispute my will'. The envelope contained the second duly executed codicil, made the same day as the first in 1908, providing that if any member of his family, being a beneficiary under his will, disputed the will or the codicil, his interests were to go to an orphanage. (The will itself had made provision for £130,000 to be used to found an orphanage in Brighton, to be named after Lady Wallace and Sir John's mother, Mrs Alicia Scott). The third codicil of April 1910 cancelled the orphanage scheme because of Sir John's disgust at an increase in the rate of death duty. It also relieved Edward Scott of his executorship, quite possibly because his health was not good.

A fourth codicil also of April 1910 cancelled the legacy of £30,000 to Lord Sackville, but only because the money had already been paid over. The fifth and final codicil of July 1910 gave the contents of Netherswell Manor to Walter and made some technical provisions about the payment of death duties.

In April 1913 the court action brought by Mr F. W. Capron, the Scott family solicitor and one of the executors, seeking to prove the will with five codicils,[1] began. Mr Capron's action was defended by all the Scott brothers and sisters who entered a defence and counterclaim that Lord and Lady Sackville had exerted undue influence on Sir John and pleaded that a further codicil (which existed in draft, see p. 99 above) had revoked the bequests to Lady Sackville and greatly reduced her benefits.[2]

Malcolm Scott had offered a reward of £10,000 to anyone who could produce the duly executed version of the codicil, but without success. Family tradition has it that Sir John Murray Scott and Lady Sackville had travelled together to Murray Lodge at Newmarket on 13 January 1912 and that after they left, a pile of ashes had been found in a fireplace, the implication being that Sir John had shown the codicil to Lady Sackville who had persuaded him to burn it. A report of the court proceedings in the *Daily Graphic* of 29 April describes the examination of Sir John's valet, Jesse Short, the purpose of which seemed to be to try to establish that Sir John always carried his will and its codicils with him wherever he went and that they would, therefore, have been with him when he visited Newmarket. The witness did not help the Scotts. He said that he was quite unaware until after Sir John's death, that an envelope marked 'private' which was kept in a locked desk drawer contained the will. He did confirm that Sir John was very particular that the envelope should always be packed when he was travelling. It would be put in a locked dressing-case:

> It was the only bag ever locked . . . It was the 'cash bag' as we called it. I gener-
> ally carried it, and if he went by motor-car it would be placed on the top,
> covered, in case it rained. It would more likely be placed on top if two or more
> people travelled in the car.

---

1 There is a copy of the will and five codicils in the Wallace Collection Archive.
2 Frederick, second Earl of Birkenhead, *F.E., The Life of F. E. Smith first Earl of Birkenhead*, Eyre & Spottiswoode, 1965, p. 191.

Although he confirmed that there were two people (Sir John Murray Scott and Lady Sackville) in the car on 13 January, he also said that as far as he was aware, no documents were carried on that occasion.

That limb of their challenge having failed, the Scotts, who had hired the almost legendary F. E. Smith (later Lord Birkenhead) as their counsel, went on to the next stage of the fight, namely their assertion that Lady Sackville had subjected Sir John to undue influence. Lady Sackville was represented by the equally famous Sir Edward Carson. It was to be a battle of the giants before Sir Samuel Evans, President of the Probate Division of the High Court, and a jury. The hearings in late June and early July 1913 caught the tail end of the London season. Society ladies queued up for seats in the court.

The whole tale of Sir John's relationship with Victoria Sackville-West was paraded in public and humiliating detail. A witness for the Scotts claimed that one day in July 1911 he had seen Victoria and Vita rummaging through Sir John's desk (the implication being that they removed and destroyed the codicil which would so drastically have reduced their share of the estate). Vita appeared on the witness stand and produced the perfect alibi. Her diary showed that on the day of the alleged incident she had been ill, and that her mother had been at home with her the whole time. She later wrote about her court appearance:

It was funny going there and seeing all Seery's family, whom I had known so well, especially his sisters, one of whom had broken to me the news of Grandpapa's death. I used to long for Seery to appear miraculously in court and tell them all what he thought of them, especially when they said that Mother and I had destroyed an unfavourable will of Seery's. I was frantic over that, and tried my best to show it when my turn came to go into the witness-box.[3]

Lady Sackville was a vivacious but extremely slippery witness. She did not answer questions put to her. She (quite improperly) wrote letters to F. E. Smith whilst the trial was going on.[4] She made the court laugh. The jury and the judge loved her. How dull the Scotts must have seemed in comparison.

The jury took only twelve minutes to find that the will and its codicils were valid. Lady Sackville had won and the Scotts had to pay her costs as well as their own, which must have been enormous.[5]

Immediately afterwards, Lady Sackville sold the contents of the rue Lafitte apart-

3 Nigel Nicolson, *Portrait of a Marriage*, Weidenfeld and Nicolson, 1973, p. 38.
4 *F.E., The Life of F. E. Smith first Earl of Birkenhead*, pp. 192–3.
5 Although Nigel Sheffield believes that F. E. Smith may have waived his fee.

Harold Nicolson (on the right) and Vita Sackville-West (in dark clothes)
arriving at the Law Courts

ment (tapestries, furniture and sculpture) *en bloc* to a Paris dealer, Jacques Seligmann. He paid her £270,000 (£15 million today, but a good deal less than the £350,000, today nearly £20 million, value that had been put on them at the trial). The first collector to buy from Seligmann was the American, Henry Frick, who had his pick before the collection had even been moved from the rue Lafitte to Seligmann's show-rooms. Frick's purchases, and many other items sold subsequently, are now to be found in museums in the United States.[6] To quote Lady Sackville's grandson, Nigel Nicolson,

6 Donald Mallett, *The Greatest Collector*, Macmillan, 1979, pp. 186, 189–90.

this was perhaps the only shameful part of the affair, for Seery (as well she knew) had hoped she would use his 'fine things' to enrich the Knole collection, not sell them to provide her with pocket-money.[7]

She bought a Rolls-Royce motor car, she bought houses; she began an entanglement with the architect Sir Edwin Lutyens, causing him quite as much heartache as she had Sir John Murray Scott; she bought new furniture and jewels for herself and for Vita. In October 1913 Vita and Harold Nicolson were married in the chapel at Knole. All twelve jurors from the case of *Capron v. Scott* were invited to the wedding.[8]

Lady Sackville probably really believed that she could make better use of the money than the Scott family, who were not, after all, related in any way to Lady Wallace. If an unkind view is taken, it could be said that Mrs Scott and her daughters cultivated their friendship with Lady Wallace with a similar, though less flamboyant, assiduity as that shown by Lady Sackville in her pursuit of Sir John. Although Lady

A family gathering at Netherswell in 1923. *From the left:* Ian (Douglas Scott's son), a nurse (Alicia Scott was by then an invalid), Mary Scott, Alicia Scott, Malcolm Scott, Bessie Scott, Douglas Scott and Lucy (Douglas's daughter)

7 *Portrait of a Marriage*, p. 71.
8 Ibid., p. 90.

Sackville's views were undoubtedly tinged with a very unattractive snobbish disdain for the middle-class Scotts, she thought that there was quite enough money for everyone, and it is hard to disagree with her. She managed to fritter most of her share away in her own lifetime, though the gifts she made to her daughter and son-in-law almost certainly enabled them to create the beautiful gardens at Sissinghurst, to which extent she can be forgiven.

One suspects that the Scotts were much more prudent. The contents of 5 Connaught Place (301 lots of furniture, porcelain, tapestries and sculpture and 153 pictures and drawings, including a number of Hertford family portraits) were sold at Christie's on 24–27 June 1913 (by coincidence 24 June was also the first day of the lawsuit).[9] Other items were disposed of in 1942 and 1943 when Mary Scott, the last of her generation, died.[10] The effects of two world wars and inflation on the country's economy in the twentieth century caused many a fortune to evaporate, so perhaps Lady Sackville was right to enjoy her inheritance while she could. She died in 1936, difficult and demanding to the last.

9 *The Greatest Collector*, pp. 187, 188.
10 *The Hertford Mawson Letters* (ed. John Ingamells), Wallace Collection, 1981, p. 19.

15

Back to Orford – Finishing Touches

There can be little doubt that the newspaper reports of the proceedings at the Royal Courts of Justice were followed avidly by Edward Scott's former parishioners and it would be interesting to know where their sympathies lay.

The next meeting of the Orford Church Restoration Committee minuted in the book was held on 7 May 1915 and seems to have been something of a 'mopping-up' exercise, which had been instigated at the Vestry Meeting that year. A letter from Edward Scott was read offering his resignation from the committee and also one from Mr Heywood, who had long since left Sudbourne Hall. There was one more meeting on 12 May with just one item of restoration business about plans that appear to have been mooted for a new screen and choir stalls. 'Letters from Mrs Jervis were read in reference to a claim made upon her by Mr Bisshopp for preparing plans and specifications for a new screen and choir stalls. After a lengthy discussion it was resolved that the matter should be discussed again after seeing Mr Clark.' (Mr Kenneth Mackenzie Clark, father of Lord Clark, see p. 10 above, was the latest owner of the Sudbourne estate, and, it would seem, was being targeted, as were his predecessors at the Hall, by the Restoration Committee.) The minute was signed off one month later by the then rector, the Revd H. A. Tudor.[1]

On 6 June 1917 Edward Scott died. His address was given in the burial register as 3 Hallam Street, Belgravia, London (although his widow continued to occupy 'Birkdale' at Branksome until 1919; she then moved to Devon). He was buried in the family plot in Orford churchyard on 9 June 1917.

---

1   The Revd Hugh A. Tudor, who became rector in 1914, had as adventurous a career as that of the Revd Cardew (see n. 3 to chapter 12 above). He was ordained in 1882 and had a curacy at Gillingham in Dorset for two years before he went to Canada where he became priest in charge of Medicine Hat, Alberta in 1884. He went on to two more Canadian parishes before returning to England to St Chad's, Everton, for just a year. In 1894 he went to South Africa where he was priest in charge of Mount Frere and then St James, Umtata. He was awarded a medal for his work as Chaplain to the Forces, 1898–1901 (during the Boer War). He worked as the organizing secretary for the Society for the Propagation of the Gospel in the diocese of Winchester from 1902 to 1904 then became vicar of Shottermill in Surrey. From 1909 to 1913 he was at Yarcombe in Devon but went for a year to be assistant chaplain at All Saints in Rome before finally settling down as rector of Sudbourne with Orford in 1914 (*Crockford's Clerical Directory*, 1915). He remained at Orford until his death in 1937.

As with all new building projects, some things were found to be in need of adjustment at Orford church. The 1912 supplemental terrier gives this information:

The long oak communion rails specified in the supplementary terrier of 1902 have been removed to the side chapel and new communion rails on brass standards affixed in their place.

The church bell having become cracked it has been taken down and one of the others substituted.

Those new communion rails did not last long. A faculty was granted in 1925 to allow for the disposal (*inter alia*) of 'Altar rails of oak and brass'. The only trace of them today is a series of marks in the stone slabs on the floor where once they were fixed.

Another relatively ephemeral item was the first of the new screens. The eighteenth-century church as re-ordered by the Revd Josiah Alsop had no rood screen. It seems that none of the medieval rood screen was kept when the work was done to wall off the Norman chancel. (The woodwork may have been rotten because of the 'decay of the partition of church and chancel' noted by the archdeacon in 1686, see p. 15 above).

Under Edward Scott's restoration scheme a new, artificial division between 'chancel' and 'nave' had to be created. In 1896 an estimate of just £25 was accepted for a rood screen, and in 1900 additional screens for the north and south aisles costing £45 were approved. They were always intended to be temporary until funds allowed for their replacement with something of a more appropriate quality. The last meeting of the restoration committee was, as we have seen, considering the matter.

When a memorial to her husband came to be chosen, Mrs Ida Scott commissioned the architect Sydney Tugwell of Bournemouth (J. T. Micklethwaite having died in 1906) to design the impressive carved oak screen which we have today. There is a fine coloured drawing of the screen design, showing metal gates which were not included in the final version. The memorial screen was carved by Lawrence Turner and completed in 1919[2] (although it was not dedicated until 1921, see below). A faculty dated 7 August 1919 was granted

(a) To remove the present temporary Screen and Rood together with the clergy and choir seats and to erect in their places a permanent carved oak Screen and Rood and oak clergy and choir stalls. (b) To fix over the Altar in the side chapel an Italian Oil Painting (believed to be the work of a pupil of Raphael) rep. The

---

2   D. P. Mortlock, *The Popular Guide to Suffolk Churches No. 3 East Suffolk*, Acorn Editions, 1992, p. 142.

Mrs Ida Scott (bottom left), Kathleen (top left) and Brida (top right) with
Loopy the dog and Ruth 'in her garden' (bottom right) in 1924

Nativity of Christ[3] (c) To erect a mural tablet in memory of Orford men who fell in the War.[4]

With the supplemental terrier of 1922 we can pick up the story of the completion of the restoration of the church fabric. We also see that the stream of donations from the Scott family continued:

Oak screen	*presented by*	Mrs Ida Marion Scott
Clergy & choir stalls		Mrs Ida Marion Scott
East window		Mrs D M Scott, Dr Maynard & Miss Maynard
'The Adoration' altar reredos in [St Nicholas] Chapel		Dr Maynard
Silver gilt chalice & patten		D. Malcolm Scott Esq.
Baptismal shell		
Font ewer		
Oak shrine		Miss Scott
Roll of Honour		
White silk offertory bags (3)		Miss Rope
Small hammered silver chalice & patten		Miss Maynard
Carved oak door		D. Malcolm Scott
Memorial cross in churchyard		public subscription
Wheeled bier		D. M. Scott
Carved oak communion rails for chapel altar		Rector Revd H. A. & Mrs Tudor

The clergy and choir stalls were designed 'in harmony with the rood screen'. The fine east window is a memorial to Mrs Louisa Maynard from her children. It was designed by J. Clement Bell and made by the well-known firm of stained glass manufacturers Clayton & Bell. It is a light and delicate work depicting the Virgin and Child in the centre with St Edmund and St Paul to the left and St Bartholomew and St Nicholas on the right. The screen, stalls and window were all dedicated at a service on All Saints' Day (1 November) 1921.[5]

3   The pupil of Raphael is Raphaelino del Colle. This was the first of two Italian old master paintings given to the church by Dr Maynard, the grandson of the former rector and brother-in-law to Malcolm Scott. In 1950 he gave the Luini which hangs above the main altar, see p. 127 below.
4   See n. 6 below.
5   *Suffolk Chronicle and Mercury*, 4 November 1921.

The nave, showing the new screen and east window

The south aisle with the screen and the altarpiece commemorating Edward Scott

The east window

The quite extraordinary generosity of Malcolm Scott is evident from the list and from other recently discovered sources. An envelope amongst the church records containing copies of the church's insurance policies has the following notes in Malcolm Scott's handwriting on it:

Insurance – Fire Burglary etc on Silver Gilt Chalice & Paten for £100. The Northern Assurance Co. Lady Day 1918. NB Premium will be paid by D. M. Scott Esq. the donor during his lifetime.

He also made a substantial contribution to the cost of the War Memorial cross,[6] said in the terrier to have been funded by public subscription. In fact the account of the

6   Although a faculty had been obtained in 1919 for a 'mural tablet' in the church to commemorate the twenty-nine Orford men who died in the First World War (out of the 141 who enlisted and whose names are on the Roll of Honour), it was decided instead to erect a War Memorial cross in the churchyard in front of the south porch.

'Cash received for Orford War Memorial Fund' shows that of the total cost of £170, only £99 was raised by public subscription.[7] The balance of £70 (£1,745 at today's values) was paid by 'M Scott Esq'.

The building works and alterations listed in the 1922 document include the undoing of some of the earlier work and the loss of the Revd and Mrs Osmund's banners:

Electric light installation, in place of the oil lamps.
Removal of communion rails on brass standards & substitution of the long oak communion rails specified in the supplementary terriers of 1902 & 1912.
Removal of wrought iron lamp standards.
Rearrangement of curtain hangings to the altar.
One (cracked) church bell removed & replaced by two of the old bells (1915).

The war memorial

7 The owners of the Sudbourne estate during the war years, Kenneth Mackenzie Clark and Walter Boynton gave £5 and 2 guineas respectively. The new owner, Joseph Watson, later Lord Manton, also gave £5.

One banner pole & two banners mentioned in the terrier July 19 1902 not found.

Roof of nave newly slated in place of lead.

Restoration of west window, partly in memory of D J Smith.[8]

Panelling of tower entrance (subscription).

Gurney heating stove.

Reparation of the Norman chancel.[9]

Plans of proposed restoration of church by George Edmund Street R.A.[10]

Repairing of windows.

Moving of font to original position.

This list includes some major work, and it also presents a puzzle. The document concludes with the usual formula showing it to be a supplemental terrier to the one taken in 1912 (the two dates, 1912 and 1922 span the creation of the new diocese of St Edmundsbury & Ipswich in 1914):

A true terrier of all the glebe & other lands, houses, tenements, tithes, rent-charges in lieu of tithes, goods, utensils, ornaments & all other rights belonging to the rectory, and the parish church of Orford in the county of Suffolk, and the diocese of St Edmundsbury and Ipswich, or given or appropriated to other pious uses in the parish, taken, made & renewed according to the old evidences and the knowledge of the ancient inhabitants; by a committee, appointed by the church council, and holden on the 11th day of February, in the year of our Lord 1922, and exhibited in the primary visitation of the right reverend father in God, Bertram, Lord Bishop of Norwich, holden at Halesworth on the 21st day of June 1912.

The problem is that the church files and account books reveal that a number of the alterations listed were carried out some time *after* 1922. The only possible explanation must be that the copy of the 1922 terrier kept in the church was continuously updated for a number of years afterwards. The writing is the same throughout the document, but the lists of items do appear to be slightly crowded into the available space.

8 See pp. 126, 127 below.

9 Yet another example of Malcolm Scott's generosity; see p. 119 below.

10 This must mean that the drawings commissioned by Sir Richard Wallace in 1881 had been given to the church (see n. 3 to chapter 6 above).

16

Slates for the Roof and Further Alterations

Whatever the explanation for that strange discrepancy, details of the alterations deserve to be given here.

First, the font. Davy recorded it in 1808 as being 'towards the west end' and he also noted that when Lord Hertford gave the organ in 1772, the organ gallery built for it nearly covered the font. A faculty was obtained in May 1922 to move the font (no mean feat) to its 'traditional' position near the entrance to the church. When that work was done, the lower step and (possibly medieval) tiles around it, which can be seen in the photograph on p. 67 above, disappeared.

Next, the replacement of the lead on the nave roof with slates, a mere twenty-five years after the whole roof had been renewed.[1]

The new roof had been the first job to be tackled in 1895–96. The fairly shallow roof of 1562 was rebuilt to the steep pitch of the fourteenth-century nave roof and had been covered with lead. By 1924 it was causing problems. A surveyor's report dated 19 February stated:

> I find that owing to the heat of the sun practically the whole of the lead on the South side . . . is slipping down and buckling in fact for about one third to half the length taken from the East end and is resting on the gutter. [The risk of the gutter collapsing and damaging the south aisle roof was pointed out.] . . . there are two very bad spots . . . the lead having buckled to such an extent as to cause an opening of roughly speaking 9 inches to 12 inches in height thus allowing the rain to drive in, numbers of the sheets have parted from the horizontal joints . . . further serious damage may ensue. My own opinion is that the pitch is far too great for a lead roof and I think you will be well advised [. . . to put on] a new roof, say of slate.

This devastating information was sent to E. E. Lofting, the Surveyor to Westminster Abbey, and successor to the architect responsible for the restoration scheme at Orford, J. T. Micklethwaite, and to Cornish & Gaymer, the builders who had carried out the work.

---

1   Papers relating to the restoration of nave roof, 1924, SRO(I) FC168/E6/4.

Left North view of the church showing the pitch of the roof before 1896, but with
the profile of the medieval roof clearly visible on the east face of the tower
Right South view showing the new steep-pitched roof with the defective lead covering

E. E. Lofting wrote back first. His letter of 20 March asserted that 'no pitch can
be said to be too steep for lead, it only wants proper fixing' and he drew a diagram
showing how the pieces of lead should be joined.

Cornish & Gaymer wrote on 16 April: 'We are very sorry to hear of the behaviour
of the lead on Orford church. It was recast and relaid in the most careful manner and
to the entire satisfaction of the architect.'

Revd Hugh A. Tudor in the Lady (now St Nicholas) chapel

By then the rector, the Revd Hugh Tudor, had sent an anguished appeal to the Diocesan Advisory Committee. His letter of 8 April said:

We have received a very grave report as to the condition of the lead covering the nave roof from Thompson & Son Building Contractors of Peterborough.

. . . it would be necessary to entirely strip the whole of the lead, recast it and relay it – in order to bring it up to 7lb a foot super which is the minimum weight it ought to be it would require an addition of some new pig lead in the casting.

The estimate for all the necessary work is £1640. We had also asked him to give us an estimate of the cost of replacing the lead with slates. His estimate after crediting the value of the old lead removed with blue slates is £360; with green slates £490.

We write to inform the Diocesan Advisory Committee and ask for early consideration as the work is a big undertaking and should be put in hand at once.

We would further inform you that this is a very fine oak roof entirely of new wood and covered with newly run lead and only erected some 25 years ago. We couldn't raise £1600 and while desirous to avoid doing anything derogatory to the archaeological character of this fine church, we feel it to be imperative to protect in as permanent a manner as possible, the building itself and the treasures it contains and this we believe will be effected by having the best quality of slate obtainable, fixed in the best possible manner . . . Modern lead is inferior to ancient and cannot be fixed to last.

We shall be grateful for any counsel the committee can give us in this grave anxiety and responsibility which has fallen on us.

A response came dated 28 April. In spite of the protestations from Westminster Abbey, the Diocesan Advisory Committee agreed with the surveyor that lead was unsuitable due to the steepness of the roof.[2] The use of slate was approved, although it was to be the more expensive green Westmoreland slate. It was made clear that Orford's was an exceptional case. Normally lead should be preserved wherever possible.

It was back to fund-raising for the congregation of St Bartholomew's. A gigantic Church Fête was held on 13 August 1924 at Sudbourne Park. The entire accounts for the event have been preserved,[3] giving the proceeds of every stall and detailing all the expenditure, right down to the purchase of the coconuts for the coconut shy. Boosted by donations of £50 from the ever-generous Malcolm Scott and £20 from Dr John

2 Whether this is the case is debatable. The roof of another Suffolk church, Dennington, is much steeper than Orford's and is lead covered.

3 Papers relating to church restoration fund, 1924–1927 (in fact they go up to 1930), SRO(I) FC168/E6/5.

Left Sam Smy, the Orford town crier, and the curate, Revd Tremgrove, at the fête
Right China stall at the fête

Maynard and Miss Maynard, a total of £227 5s 11d was raised (nearly £7,000 in today's money).

In the event, it was more than enough to cover the re-roofing which was completed by the end of the year. The bill from Wm C. Reade of Aldeburgh, who did the work, was for £718 4s 6d, but the church was credited with £623 1s 9d for the old lead, so the rescue operation cost only £95 2s 9d and that included additional works. The south aisle roof was releaded, flashings, gutters and gutter boards were renewed and some leaded lights were repaired.

The rood and other screens which had been replaced in 1919 by the oak screen in memory of Edward Scott were not immediately discarded. They were revealed for what they were in the faculty (mentioned on p. 108 above) dated 17 November 1925, which allowed the disposal of:

1. Screen of deal, painted green. 2. Glass formerly in east window of chancel.
3. harmonium. 4. Altar rails of oak and brass. 5. Three large panels of wood
painted with Lord's Prayer etc [thus leaving only the pictures of Moses and
Aaron from the eighteenth-century reredos]. 6. Two metal lamp standards.

The other interesting item in the supplemental terrier is the 'reparation of the
Norman chancel'. The pre-1896 photographs show brick work repairs to the Norman
columns. An archaeological excavation was undertaken by F. H. Fairweather in 1930
and reported in the *Antiquaries' Journal*. R. A. Roberts, the then churchwarden, in a
scholarly little church guide-book called *'Oreford-nigh-the-seas'* written and published
in 1935, reproduced the archaeological report[4] and wrote of 'the generosity of a
benefactor, a member of a family long intimately connected with both church and
town [which has enabled the ruins to be] made sound and weatherproof for the time
to come'.[5] The church account books for 1930, now in the Suffolk Record Office,
reveal that donor to be Mr D. M. Scott, who gave £187 9s for 'the restoration of the
arches'.[6] A letter dated 2 September 1930 to R. A. Roberts from the diocesan

The ruins of the Norman chancel before restoration

4 R. A. Roberts, *'Oreford-Nigh-the-Seas'*, Richard Clay, Bungay, 1935, Appendix II, p. 63.
5 Ibid., p. 18.
6 SRO(I) FC168/E6/5.

Malcolm and Bessie Scott at Great House on the day of their silver wedding in 1923 with
their daughter Alice Katherine (always called Gillie). Gillie married the Revd Digby
Sheffield. Their son Nigel Sheffield has provided a great deal of the information about the
Maynard and Scott families and the family photographs used in this book.

architect, H. Munro Cautley, who had overseen the work and whose fee of 12 guineas
had also been paid by Malcolm Scott, summed things up well: 'Mr Scott is a wonderful man, and it is most extraordinarily generous of him.'

As with the slating of the roof, the mystery is why it and the work on the ruins are
listed in the 1922 terrier when the actual dates of the work were 1924 and 1930
respectively.

There is a hangover from the episode of the pews (recounted in chapter 11, p. 85
above) to be found in R. A. Roberts's book. He describes the appearance of the church
in the eighteenth century, and says:

:eats then found in the church, the only remaining examples are, prob-
se now serving in the [St Nicholas] Chapel. When it was thought fit to
seating of the church, to abolish pews most suited to a country parish
tion, and imitate Cathedral conditions with moveable chairs for casual
ers, these with all other pews were cast out to the limbo of the picker-
ere recovered by Mr. Crisp, a member of an old resident family, and
ɔ use in the church in 1914.

l pulpit with its canopy followed the pews on to the scrap heap. Pieces
ɔised but useful seating accommodation for a country parish congre-
said to be found here and there in the parish, adapted to some form
ld furniture.[7]

still rankled thirty-four years later although it seems to have been for-
that the pews which were rescued and reinstated were not the medieval
iteenth-century box pews but the pews in the south aisle which had
he Revd John Maynard who had died in 1877. The sale by auction
e members of the restoration committee had become in folk memory
:king-out, and the reference to cathedrals would seem to be a side-
cklethwaite's connection with Westminster Abbey.

---

7 It is true that some woodwork was salvaged. Mrs Molly Keer, whose grandfather, William Gibbs, was a carpenter who worked on the restoration (see p. 88 above), remembers a cupboard in her family home which was made from the old pews.

17

The Tower – A Project of the Twentieth Century

The one part of the church that was not included in Edward Scott's programme of works was the ruined tower. In the letter he wrote to the Incorporated Church Building Society in June 1899 (see p. 80 above) he said that he wished to see the completion of the repair of 'the whole church bar the tower'. In fact £18 was spent on the tower floor in the first phase of the restoration (see p. 71 above), and the tower entrance was panelled between 1912 and 1922 (see p. 114 above). Nevertheless it seems a pity to leave this account of the church restoration without mentioning the troublesome tower which probably gave more of a headache to the churchwardens of St Bartholomew's than anything else for nearly three hundred years.

In the eighteenth century the tower seems to have been as much of a problem at the west end of the church as the Norman chancel was in the east (see pp. 15, 16 above).

A petition to the bishop dated 28 April 1706 describes the church as being 'decay'd both within and without' then continues:

> and moreover the Tower of ye said church (which is very high and large), and which by reason of its situation near Orford-ness is by all accounted ye most considerable Sea Mark in Europe for avoiding many dangerous sands, upon the decay of wch. ye Navigation to Newcastle, and between England and Holland and to all ye Northern parts of ye world be very much endangered and obstructed, and ye said Tower being now decay'd on ye top and crack'd half way down does require speedy care and great expence, to repair and strengthen it . . .[1]

Two years later another petition was submitted requesting permission to demolish the chancel, but it was followed by a list of 'things necessary to be done to Orford church and Tower' which would seem to indicate that nothing had been done in spite of the urgency of the earlier petition. The benefaction boards recording sums given and detailing some of the work carried out make no mention of the tower.

A Vestry meeting of 21 August 1739 records that it was 'agreed that the upper part of

---

1 L. Dow, 'Orford Church in 1706', *Proceedings of the Suffolk Institute of Archaeology*, vol. 26 (1952–54), p. 225.

Print of Orford church and Church Street, *c.* 1815. The large house on the left became
Great House, the home of the Maynards (see pp. 39 and 41 above).

the steeple which is now in a ruinous repair, shall be immediately rectified and repaired'.

If that work was done, it did not stand the test of time. The archdeacon's visitation letter in 1788 makes alarming reading and was carefully copied into the front of
the churchwardens' account book:

> Top part of south parapet of Tower extremely bad, wants coping, a number of
> scaffold holes on South Side Tower. South west turret to repair at top. Second
> set-off of buttress to ditto [i.e. to the south-west turret] wants much repair,
> bottom of south side of tower wants underpinning. West battlements of tower
> very bad . . . North side of tower, a large settlement crack over north window.
> West end of North isle to point . . . earth to remove from North sides . . .[2]

The *Ipswich Journal* of 18 May 1830 contains the following paragraph:

2 Churchwardens' Book containing disbursements 1744–1789, SRO(I) FC168/E5/1.

Orford steeple. This ancient edifice and noted sea-mark gave way a short time since, when one of the buttresses fell, leaving a considerable fissure in the centre. Early on Sunday morning last the greater part came down with a tremendous crash.

It seems clear that the disaster happened in two stages. Early in April a buttress fell. The Vestry minutes of 13 April record a resolution that the churchwardens should put the steeple into thorough repair. The rector, the Revd John Connor, lost no time in putting pen to paper. His letter is to be found in the earliest Orford church file in the Incorporated Church Building Society's archive.[3] It is addressed 'To the Incorporated Society for promoting the Enlargement Building and Repairing of Churches and Chapels, No. 2 Parliament Street, Westminster, London', and reads:

> At a Vestry Meeting held this 13th day of April 1830 in the Church of Orford in the county of Suffolk, it is agreed by us the Minister Churchwardens and principal Inhabitants of the Parish to petition you Gentlemen in humbly requesting that you will be pleased to have the Goodness to assist us with some money to repair our Church which is in a dilapidated State in the Walls and Roof, in so much so that Part of the Steeple of the church fell down last friday night in the Time of a great Tempest we had, attended with Lightening and Thunder, and the Parishioners in general are very poor and cannot afford to do the Repairs of the Church without some Relief from you, which in your Goodness we hope you will grant us and your Petitioners will ever pray.

The petition is signed by the rector, the two churchwardens, Daniel Kerridge and F. Keer, and five inhabitants, George Randall, Wm Field, John Pope, Christopher Churchill and Samuel Randall. It is endorsed 'Sent Queries'.

Before any further steps were taken, there was the second and much more damaging fall. According to R. A. Roberts,[4] a manuscript memorandum by an Orford resident at that time reads:

> May 9th, 1830. About ¼ past 8 a.m. (just after the man who tolled the 8 o'clock bell had quitted the church) the S.E. angle of Orford steeple fell, it having been in a dilapidated and unsafe condition for upward of thirty years.

The same issue of the *Ipswich Journal* that carried the report of the incident also has an advertisement:

---

3 ICBS file 1226, Lambeth Palace Library.
4 R. A. Roberts, *'Oreford-Nigh-the-Seas'*, Richard Clay, Bungay, 1935, pp. 24, 25.

The tower as it looked for about a hundred and thirty years

Any persons willing to contract for taking down the tower of Orford Church with the bells and bell frames may view the plan by applying to Mr. Daniel Kerridge, Churchwarden. Tenders to be delivered in on or before the 20th of May. — Orford, May 13th, 1830.

In July, an agreement signed by twelve of the principal householders is recorded in the Vestry minutes that a contract should be entered into for the repair of the tower for £81. The tower was patched up and left in the state familiar to us from all the early photographs. Happily, the interesting medieval stair leading from the first stage (the ringing chamber) to the second stage, where the clock is, was undamaged.

Four bells were brought down and placed on the floor at the back of the church. One of them was rehung in place of the single bell that had been left and which had become cracked, as recorded in the 1912 supplemental terrier.

At the time when it seems funds were not available to rebuild the tower, the rector, the Revd John Jenkinson, who was appointed in January 1832, took out a mortgage for £920 to rebuild the rectory,[5] described by Davy as 'an entire new Parsonage House

---

5 Mortgage for the purpose of rebuilding the rectory, 4 June 1832, SRO(I) FC168/C9/1. The architect was Matthew Hastings of Eynsham, Oxfordshire.

Window commemorating D. J. Smith

but upon the site of the old one . . . facing the south. It is externally a very neat look-ing building.'[6]

We have noted the work that was done to the floor and walls of the tower as part of the 'Scott' restoration. In 1928 the stonework of the west tower window was repaired and a stained-glass panel inserted showing the arms of the borough of Orford and the inscription:

To the glory of God and in memory of David James Smith, benefactor of the Church and Poor of Orford, born in the town, 8th April 1856, died at sea 7th May 1915 when the S.S. *Lusitania* was sunk by an enemy submarine.

D. J. Smith was born in Orford but spent most of his life travelling in Europe and America as a valet. He saved his money and maybe made some shrewd investments because, after his untimely death, he was found to have left quite a substantial sum to the rector and churchwardens of Orford to set up two charities. One was for the poor of the parish, to whom coal was to be distributed each year, and the other was to set up a fund to be used for the ornamentation of the church, expressing a particular wish that a stained-glass window should be inserted 'to make it beautiful'.

6 *Collection for the History of Suffolk by Hundreds and Parishes*, British Library Add MSS 19077-19113 (microfilm in SRO (I)).

A sack of coal was given to almost every old person in the village each year from 1916 right up to the Second World War. By the end of the twentieth century, however, the capital value of the fund had so diminished that it took five years' income to pay for one load of coal for the last beneficiary. The fund for the ornamentation of the church has fared better, and still produces enough income to make it a useful source of money for minor repairs and improvements.[7]

At the same time that the work was done on the west window, the west door was replaced. The new door was designed by Hilda Mason, a woman architect who did some interesting work in Suffolk in the 1920s and 1930s, including Green Lane House in Orford and the remarkable St Andrew's church in Felixstowe (the first church in England to use ferro-concrete as the basic material, and, it must be said, now suffering severe structural problems).[8] The oak tower door for St Bartholomew's was carved by members of Archdeacon Darling's guild of carvers from the nearby village of Eyke[9] and assembled by William Large, the wheelwright in Butley. Yet again it was Malcolm Scott who paid for Orford's new carved door.

In 1935 the churchwarden R. A. Roberts wrote his little history and guide book and commented that the tower arch was at that time, 'temporarily, it is to be hoped, filled with plain, blue painted boarding'.[10]

As for the rest of the church, the programme of restoration turned into one of repair and maintenance. A highlight in 1950 was Dr Maynard's gift of the painting of the Italian School, *The Holy Family with St John and a Donor* by Bernardino Luini (active 1512, died 1532), which hangs above the altar.[11]

In the 1960s the restoration of the tower began, when it was raised to just above

7 D. J. Smith Charities' files held by the churchwardens. In 2005 the charities were wound up under a scheme approved by the Charity Commission.

8 Raymond Erith collaborated with Hilda Mason at Felixstowe, D. P. Mortlock, *The Popular Guide to Suffolk Churches No. 3 East Suffolk*, Acorn Editions, 1992, pp. 63–4.

9 Ibid, pp. 61, 141. James Darling was rector of Eyke from 1893 to 1939 and taught wood carving to the villagers. They became skilled craftsmen. There is a great deal of their work in Eyke church, but also in other churches in the district.

10 'Oreford-Nigh-the-Seas', p. 35.

11 For details of the painting see the abbreviated, revised and re-edited version of 'Oreford-Nigh-the-Seas' published by the Rector and Churchwardens in 1958 and used for many years as the church guide book, 1973 reprint, pp. 11, 12. A letter in the church files from W. A. Martin, a director of Christie's, the art auctioneers, dated 3 April 1956 and written to Major Steuart Gratton the church-warden (who had been seeking an insurance valuation for the Luini), says 'In confidence, I may tell you that Dr Maynard paid no more than 100 guineas for it . . . he was an old habitué of Christie's and I myself knew him for a good 25 years. When he bought the picture, we thought it was a very good buy and something in the nature of a discovery . . .' The cleaning and restoration of the picture in 1956 cost £150, more than had been paid for its purchase. A grant of £15 was obtained from The National Art Collections Fund. It has to be said that the picture, even after cleaning, is very obscure.

Dr Maynard and Miss Maynard mowing the lawn at Great House, 1920s

the level of the ridge of the nave roof thanks to a bequest of £7,500 from Dr Maynard's sister, Miss Maynard.

The following decade saw the tower completed to its full height to plans by the architect Bruce George and at a cost of £10,500, work which was assisted by a grant from the Incorporated Church Building Society. The driving force behind the project again came from the rectory, which by the 1960s had become The Old Rectory. The churchwarden, William Servaes, who was General Administrator of the Aldeburgh Festival, lived there, and, with his fellow churchwarden, Major John Steuart Gratton (a keen amateur archaeologist, whose work paved the way for the opening of Orford Museum), they saw through the rebuilding of the troublesome tower which at last stands firm. Their achievement is rightly commemorated on a lead plaque by the tower arch bearing their initials, the date and the words *Laus Deo*.[12]

The project was triumphantly completed in 1999 with the creation of a choir vestry with cupboards and a sink on the ground floor, a ringing chamber reached by a new spiral stair, the repair and rehanging of the old bells and the casting of new ones to make a complete ring for the new Millennium. R. A. Roberts's wish for the tower arch ('Here is an opportunity for some future benefactor to remove this

12 *'Oreford-Nigh-the-Seas'*, 1973 reprint, p. 7.

unsightly structure and replace it with a suitable screen and doorway') was fulfilled when the new wood and glass screen, which gracefully echos the design of the rood screen, was inserted. The new ringing chamber, the west tower window and the medieval staircase are all now visible through the top of the arch. The architect was Andrew Anderson, and one of the churchwardens involved was Tim Fargher, the artist, son-in-law of William Servaes and his successor at The Old Rectory.

The ringing chamber, the west window and part of the medieval stair

18

The Work Continues

So what should be the verdict on the restoration of Orford church?

In 1892 the building clearly was in imminent danger of collapse. As we have seen, Larner Sugden (see pp. 61, 62 above) was far from the mark in 1894 when he described the nave and north aisle as 'the glorious portion of the fabric which remains as yet intact and almost as its gifted creators left it'. The church had undergone tremendous change over the centuries.

The ambitious plans of G. E. Street came closest to those of the 'gifted creators' when he proposed reincorporating the Norman chancel into the building, but even he refrained from suggesting the rebuilding of the central tower. Those plans came to nothing, probably because even someone of Sir Richard Wallace's wealth would have found the scheme eye-wateringly costly. The present generation should be grateful that they do not have the responsibility for the upkeep of such an enormous structure, had the work been carried out.

The architect who did undertake the restoration, J. T. Micklethwaite, can be credited with a sensitive and sensible scheme which seems generally to have made the best of what remained of the work of the successive generations of 'creators' who had contributed to the appearance of the church. In particular, he uncovered the Norman stonework in the north-east corner, which had been concealed when the new east wall was made in the early eighteenth century. This, ironically, was achieved by flying in the face of one of the precepts of the Society for the Protection of Ancient Buildings, whose informal name was the 'Anti-Scrape'. The SPAB was averse to the scraping away of old wall surfaces and their replacement with smooth new plaster, partly because there was a risk that wall paintings and other interesting features could be destroyed, but also on aesthetic grounds.

A faint flavour of the appearance of the interior of the medieval church with its chapels, each with their own altar, can still be detected by the remaining piscinas and niches in the walls at both the east and west ends of the church. There is documentary evidence, too. Altars and 'tabernacles' dedicated to many different saints, a painted candle beam and gilding on the font are mentioned in the surviving wills of Orford's pre-Reformation inhabitants.[1]

1   V. B. Redstone, 'The Sandling, III Orford', *Proceedings of the Suffolk Institute of Archaeology*, vol. x (1898), pp. 89–92.

The north-east corner of Orford Church in the 1930s

We should be glad that no attempt was made to put coloured glass back into the nave windows after William Dowsing 'brake down 28 superstitious pictures' (which were almost certainly stained-glass windows). That decision, and the unblocking of the clerestory windows, which means that Orford church is full of light, is to be applauded.

It is permissible to lament the loss of the west gallery and of the Revd Josiah Alsop's scheme of arrangement. He tried, and, it seems, largely succeeded in transforming a medieval country church into something resembling one of Christopher Wren's churches in the City of London – quite an achievement.

The nineteenth century saw a great change in the liturgical practices of the Church of England, and we have seen that the appearance of the south aisle was almost certainly being altered before the Revd Edward Scott arrived on the scene. The decision to insert a rood screen across the church, thus breaking up the fine space of the nave and aisles, although understandable in the light of the thinking of the time,[2] is perhaps the only one to be deplored.

There is also a suspicion (see Larner Sugden's remarks about ancient carved seats, and C. R. B. Barrett's sketch, p. 65 above), that some interesting woodwork may have been lost. We have no idea of the quality of the woodwork in the roof of the fourteenth-century nave and aisles – it had been replaced in 1562, and J. T. Micklethwaite's new roof is certainly finer than that one was. There seems to be re-use of an old parclose screen of the fifteenth or sixteenth century to separate the sanctuary from the side chapels, and the bases of those partitions and the panelling separating the choir from the St Nicholas chapel may include wood from the eighteenth-century box pews. On the north side of the choir the very handsome screen in front of the organ, bearing the royal arms of William and Mary (1689–1702), which was once part of the corporation pew, has been retained, almost *in situ*, judging by Emmeline Rope's picture (see p. 63 above). There is also an interesting and ancient ladder stair leading from the ringing chamber up into the tower. This adds up to a reasonable tally of survival.

On the whole, the result is very satisfactory, and all subsequent work has maintained or enhanced the appearance of the church as the restorers left it.

The church has an exceptionally fine acoustic which together with the flexible seating arrangements makes it very suitable for concerts and recording. We have seen

2 There was greater emphasis on ritual and ceremonial, and the eucharist (Holy Communion) was celebrated every Sunday instead of just three or four times a year. The 'holiness' of the altar was accentuated by being raised up on steps, and it was set apart from the rest of the church in a sanctuary beyond the altar rails at the end of a chancel (the area reserved for the clergy and choir). As Orford had lost its chancel, a new area to serve as a chancel had to be created by the insertion of a screen to separate off the two most easterly bays of the church.

(p. 73 above) how Benjamin Britten appreciated those qualities, and the church is still regularly used for concerts during the Aldeburgh Festival. Income from recordings made a significant contribution towards meeting the cost of the Millennium tower project. The annual bazaar, coffee mornings, sales, art shows, the harvest supper and exhibitions mounted by Orford Museum all nowadays take place in the church.

From time to time the work recommended as a result of the architect's quinquennial inspection is so substantial as to turn it into a full-blown restoration project. This was the case following the report by Tony Redman of the Whitworth Co-Partnership, an architectural practice of Bury St Edmunds, in 2002.

The most obvious indications that all was not well were the failure of the church's central-heating boiler, leaks in the roofs of both north and south aisles and the failure of the soakaways linked to the rainwater downpipes to do their job. In addition, the alarming information that the 'cores' of several of the external buttresses had been washed out as a result of water penetration so that they were effectively hollow, prompted yet another restoration campaign. The Parochial Church Council was also anxious to comply, so far as practicable, with the requirements of the legislation about access to buildings by disabled people.

Under the determined direction of Canon Robert Clifton (rector from 1995 to 2005) it was decided that there would be a two-year period in which to raise £200,000 to allow for all those works and the internal redecoration of the church to be undertaken. A combination of an energetic programme of fund-raising events (some very similar to those of 1894, though concerts organized by Music in Country Churches took the place of the 'Jimcrack Minstrels', and instead of the church fête of 1924, a May Fair and a Giant Flea Market were held) and successful applications to some of the grant-giving bodies that over the course of the twentieth century have largely taken the place of wealthy individuals as sources of funding, resulted in the completion of all the planned works on time and within budget. The target sum was actually reached and slightly exceeded in eighteen months.

Firm and level vehicular access was constructed from the Market Square gates to the north door (which has been adapted for disabled access) and to the south porch. When exploratory work was done to investigate the subsurface of the grassy path leading south from the porch to the gates on to High Street, a handsome cobbled path with stone edging was uncovered – a long-hidden legacy of the Revd Edward Scott's restoration. With a new iron handrail to one side, it is now fully revealed and back in use.

The installation of a new boiler and radiators, roof repairs and the consolidation of the buttresses, all very necessary but relatively 'unshowy' work, was done. More obviously pleasing has been the redecoration which greatly enhances the light and airy interior of the church. In addition, some stonework at the base of the piers was

The south path

renewed and the limewash removed from the Norman stonework in the north-east wall, enabling the fine architectural detail to be seen.

This particularly lovely corner of the church, known in the fifteenth century as the Chapel of Our Lady in the Wall and later as the Mayor's Chapel, had become the priest's vestry, with a sink in one corner and the boiler flue and safe as prominent features. The work on the tower for the Millennium had included the creation of a new choir vestry, freeing the former choir vestry in the north aisle behind the organ for a priest's vestry. As part of the latest restoration, the twentieth-century clutter was removed from the chapel and the decision was made that it should revert to the medieval dedication.

The south-east chapel, which had been the Lady Chapel for about one hundred years, at least since the completion of the 'Scott' restoration, has been rededicated to St Nicholas. This had an historical precedent in that the will dated 1 May 1474 of Collette, wife of John Hankyn of Orford, who had a house in the Market Square, requested that she be buried in the 'chancel of St Nicholas of Orford' and left money for 'the reparation of the tabernacle of St Bartholomew of the said church', leading to speculation that the church's dedication was changed for a while to St Nicholas. As he is the sailor's saint, and fishing and the coastal trade were so important to medieval Orford, this is not completely implausible. St Nicholas is depicted in the right hand panel of the east window (see p. 112 above).

The completion of the latest restoration campaign was celebrated at a Service of Thanksgiving and Rededication on Saturday 5 February 2005 led by the bishop of St Edmundsbury and Ipswich, the Right Reverend Richard Lewis. It also coincided with Canon Robert Clifton's retirement.

In his sermon, the bishop commented on the fact that when he visited churches for services, he was often seated on his own at the east end, a long way from the members of the congregation, and he had ample opportunity to read the memorial slabs on the walls and in the floors. (At Orford he could not have failed to notice the name of the Revd Edward Scott).

The result is a rather wonderful picture of the people who have nurtured and cared for our churches through the ages . . . I often wonder what people will read about us on the walls of our churches when they look at them in two, three, four and five hundred years time . . . I think we are fairly self-effacing and there is currently a move away from putting memorials on church walls anyway. But I think that the buildings themselves will be the evidence and people will look back to the end of the twentieth century and the beginning of the Third Millennium and they will say, 'What was happening at that point in history?', because churches were never better cared for in the whole of history than at that time. They will wonder what we were about and why we did it. You might want to ponder on that too because you are a part of the extraordinary history of this place and you have done great works in your generation.

The many reminders of the Scott family in St Bartholomew's church are indeed far from self-effacing, but now that we know something of their story and the story of the more reticent Maynards, it can be seen that the history of this church is all the more extraordinary for their contribution to it.

Bibliography

All Saints' Church, Branksome Park, a brief history of the church, 1990, revised 1999

Allen, Jane, 'The search for the hospital of St Leonard', *Orford & District Local History Bulletin*, Issue 6, 2006, p. 9

Anderson, John , 'Danger – River Ore!', *Orford & District Local History Bulletin*, Issue 7, 2006, p. 2

Barrett's Illustrated Guides: Suffolk Coast No. 2, Aldeburgh, Leiston, Orford, Butley, Lawrence & Bullen, 1892

Birkenhead, Frederick, second Earl of, *F.E., The Life of F. E. Smith first Earl of Birkenhead*, Eyre & Spottiswoode, 1965

Burke's Peerage and Baronetage, 1912, 'Scott of Castle House'

Burns, F., 'The Life and Work of Sir Richard Wallace Bart. MP', *Lisburn Historical Society Journal*, vol. 3, 1980

Cautley, H. Munro, *Suffolk Churches and their Treasures*, first published 1937, 4th rev. edn, The Boydell Press, 1975

Clark, Kenneth, 'The Other Side of the Alde', in *Tribute to Benjamin Britten on his Fiftieth Birthday*, Anthony Gishford (ed.), Faber and Faber, 1963

– *Another Part of the Wood*, John Murray, 1974

Clodd, H. P., *Aldeburgh, the History of an Ancient Borough*, Norman Adlard, 1959

Cooper, Trevor (ed.), *The Journal of William Dowsing*, Ecclesiological Society and The Boydell Press, 2001

Copinger, W. A., *Manors of Suffolk*, Manchester, 1905–11, vol. v

Crabbe, Revd George, *Crabbe's Life and Poems*, 1834, vol. 1

Creevey, Thomas, *The Creevey Papers*, Sir Herbert Maxwell (ed.), John Murray, 1903

Crockford's Clerical Directory, 1877, 1909, 1915

Davy, David Elisha, *Collection for the History of Suffolk by Hundreds and Parishes*, British Library Add. MSS 19077–19113

Dixon, Hugh, 'Aspects of the legacy of Sir Richard Wallace in the fabric of Lisburn', *Lisburn Historical Society Journal*, vol. 4, 1982

Dow, L., 'Orford Church in 1706', *Proceedings of the Suffolk Institute of Archaeology*, vol. 26 (1952–54), p. 225

Fairweather, F. H., 'Excavations in the ruined Choir of the Church of St Bartholomew, Orford, Suffolk', *Antiquaries Journal*, c. 1931, reproduced as Appendix II in Roberts, R. A., 'Oreford-Nigh-the-Seas', see below

Falk, Bernard, *"Old Q's" Daughter*, Hutchinson, 1937

Farrer, Edmund, *List of Suffolk Brasses*, 1903

Fleming, Patricia Harvey, *Villagers and Strangers, an English Proletarian Village over Four Centuries*, Schenken Publishing Company, 1979

Glendinning, Victoria, *Vita, The Life of V. Sackville-West*, Weidenfeld & Nicolson, 1983

Harrison, Matthew, *An Anglican Adventure, The History of Saint George's Anglican Church, Paris*, Saint George's Anglican Church, 2005

Harrup, Vic, 'The Buckle family of Orford at a time of religious change,' *Orford & District Local History Bulletin*, Issue 7, 2006, p. 11

Harrup, Vic, 'Captain's Wood, Sudbourne', *Orford & District Local History Bulletin*, Issue 6, 2006, p. 1

Hibbert, Christopher, *George IV*, Allen Lane, 1975

Hoey, Lawrence R., and Thurlby, Malcolm, 'A survey of Romanesque vaulting in Great Britain and Ireland', *Antiquaries Journal*, vol. 84, 2004, pp. 117–84

Hughes, Peter, *The Founders of the Wallace Collection*, Wallace Collection, 1981

Ingamells, John (ed), *The Hertford Mawson Letters*, Wallace Collection, 1981

– *The 3rd Marquess of Hertford as a Collector*, Wallace Collection, 1983

An illustrated catalogue of some of the articles in church furniture manufactured by Jones & Willis, 57th edn, Birmingham and London, 1875

Kelly's Directory, Bournemouth, Dorset, 1911, 1915

Kelly's Directory of Suffolk, 1892

Mallett, Donald, *The Greatest Collector*, Macmillan, 1979

Martin, Edward, 'Chillesford Lodge: a nineteenth century model farm', *Orford & District Local History Bulletin*, Issue 5, 2005, p. 1

Martin, Joanna, 'Ecclesiastical Jurisdictions', *An Historical Atlas of Suffolk* (David Dymond and Edward Martin (eds.)), Suffolk County Council, 3rd edn, rev. and enlarged, 1999

Middleton-Stewart, Judith, 'Down to the sea in ships: decline and fall on the Suffolk coast', *Counties and Communities, Essays on East Anglian History presented to Hassell Smith*, Centre of East Anglian Studies, University of East Anglia, 1996

Montebianco, Roland, *Sir Richard Wallace: Cet illustre inconnu*, Editions Didier Carpentier, 2007

Mortlock, D. P., *The Popular Guide to Suffolk Churches No. 3 East Suffolk*, Acorn Editions, 1992

Nicolson, Nigel, *Portrait of a Marriage*, Weidenfeld & Nicolson, 1973

Page, William (ed.), *The Victoria County History of the Counties of England: Suffolk*, Constable & Co. (1907), vol. II

Poulter, Margaret, *The Rope Family of Orford*, booklet published by Orford Museum, 1998

Redstone, V. B., 'The Sandling, III Orford', *Proceedings of the Suffolk Institute of Archaeology*, vol. X (1898), p. 89

– 'Orford and its Castle', *Proceedings of the Suffolk Institute of Archaeology*, vol. X, p. 204

– 'The Suffolk Shore', *Memorials of Old Suffolk*, Bemrose & Sons, 1908

Report of the Commission of Inquiry Concerning Charities, ordered to be printed 1829, entry on Orford, Suffolk

Riches, Anne, *Victorian Church Building and Restoration in Suffolk*, a supplement to H. Munro Cautley's *Suffolk Churches*, The Boydell Press, 1982

Roberts, R. A., 'In the Spacious Days at Orford', *East Anglian Daily Times*, 28 December 1932

– (The Rector's Warden), *'Oreford-Nigh-the-Seas'*, Richard Clay, Bungay, 1935

Scarfe, Norman, *The Suffolk Landscape*, Phillimore, new edn, 2002

– 'St Bartholomew's Church, Orford', article in concert programme, Music in Country Churches, 2003

Sudbourn and Orford Parish Magazine, June and September 1888

The Suffolk Traveller, Topographical and Historical Description of the County of Suffolk, Woodbridge, 1829

Thackeray, William Makepeace, *Vanity Fair*, 1847–48

Tricker, Roy, *All Saints Church Sudbourne Suffolk, a brief history and guide*, 1987

Watson, Sir Francis, 'The Great Wood Party', *Apollo Magazine*, CXXXI, June 1965, pp. 480–81

Wayman, H. W. B., *The Monumental Inscriptions Remaining in the Church of St Bartholomew at Orford in Suffolk*, English Monumental Inscriptions Society, 1911

– [H. W. B. W.], *Suffolk Wills (Orford) proved in the Prerogative Court of Canterbury Between 1383 and 1800*, Poole and Pemberton for the English Monumental Inscriptions Society, 1915

Webster, C., and Elliott, J. (eds.), *'A Church as it should be', the Cambridge Camden Society and its influence*, Shaun Tyas, 2000

Wentworth Day, James, 'Comment', *East Anglian Magazine*, vol. 25 no. 12 (October 1966), p. 402

White's Directory of Suffolk, 1844, 1874

Williamson, Tom, *Sandlands: The Suffolk Coast and Heaths*, Windgather Press, 2005

Wilson, Harriette, *Memoirs*, 1825, reprinted by Peter Davies, 1929

Index

References are to page numbers and may include footnotes on that page. Where the number is followed by the letter n, the reference is only to a footnote. Numerals in *italics* refer to illustrations; *f* is the frontispiece.